American Dish

100 Recipes
From Ten Delicious Decades

Merrill Shindler

Design by
Samuels Darnall & Associates

Calligraphy & Illustrations by
Lisa Holtzman

ACP
ANGEL CITY PRESS
SANTA MONICA

ANGEL CITY PRESS, INC.
Published by Angel City Press
2118 Wilshire Boulevard, Suite 880
Santa Monica, California 90403
(310) 395-9982

First published in 1996 by Angel City Press
1 3 5 7 9 10 8 6 4 2
FIRST EDITION
ISBN 1-883318-10-6

AMERICAN DISH
Copyright © 1996 by Merrill Shindler
Designed by Samuels Darnall & Associates
Lettering and Illustrations by Lisa Holtzman
Recipes authenticated by master chef Emerson Holmes

Library of Congress Cataloging-in-Publication Data

Shindler, Merrill.
    American dish : 100 recipes from ten delicious decades /
by Merrill Shindler. —1st ed.
        p.   cm.
    Includes bibliographical references and index.
    ISBN 1-883318-10-6 (cloth)

    1. Cookery, American. 2. Cookery—
United States—History—20th century.   I. Title.
TX715.S55815 1996
641.5973—dc20   96-25319
                                            CIP

Printed in the United States of America.

To Jean and Paddy for asking.

And to Merri and Jed for putting up
with all the leftovers.

Contents

Introduction

Looking at the twentieth century with twenty-twenty hindsight, it can be argued that this has been the single most remarkable century in the history of getting a bite to eat. Prior to this century, the way things worked with regard to food was pretty simple. The rich indulged their culinary taste however they wanted, living a fine life on pheasant and grouse, river salmon and trout, wines of distinction and desserts of decadence. The rest of us ate pretty much whatever we could get our hands on. For not just the lower classes but for the middle class as well, dinner was the stew pot, the mulligan, the goulash, the ragout, the salmagundi.

It's been said that prior to the twentieth century, Americans ate only three vegetables — and two of them were cabbage. Voltaire's famous observation that the English have forty-two religions but only two sauces could easily be transferred to Americans on the cusp of the 1900s. As a nation, we did not eat well. As the Comte de Volney observed at about that time, "I will venture to say that if a prize were proposed for the scheme of a regimen most calculated to injure the stomach, the teeth and the health in general, no better could be invented than that of the Americans."

Then along came the twentieth century. And through a combination of pluck, ambition, good ol' American know-how, inventiveness and the desire to make a buck at it, food became big business in these United States. The seemingly ubiquitous cereal-advocate John Harvey Kellogg kicked off the century with his dire warnings on the dangers of eating meat, of not chewing your food often enough, of eating sugar and of failing to endure a minimum of one colonic a day (and far more if the system was out of whack). He was against sex as well, feeling that it sapped the body of its vital fluids and purity of essence. Naturally, the fact that he raged against the pleasures of the flesh — culinary and otherwise — made untold thousands who heard his lectures hunger for a taste of beef, pork, lamb and chicken. What we were warned against was what we most wanted. So the inhabitants of the early twentieth century got busy eating. And their offspring kept the faith

— the twentieth century has been a hundred-year-long all-you-can-eat buffet.

The more I learn about the history of food and the corresponding world of food in history, however, the more convinced I grow that it's written on Jell-O. There's very little in culinary history that can be nailed down absolutely; it's the most non-linear form of history imaginable. It's hardly even cyclical. If anything, it's random and arbitrary, with no imaginable way of stating when and where the first tuna noodle casserole or turkey meat loaf was conceived and then consumed. Like Athena from the head of Zeus, most culinary innovations seem to have emerged fully formed. One day they didn't exist, and the next day everyone was making them. The Food Stork brought them.

Which is why this decade-by-decade history of American eating and drinking habits is a book of informed opinion. I'm not suggesting that the recipes included in each decade were born in that decade, though in many cases that's true. What I'm dealing with here is an impression of food history: the dishes assigned to each decade are indicative of the culinary life of that era. There's something about baked Alaska and oysters Rockefeller that speaks volumes about the 1900s; onion dip and cheese fondue are very much the 1950s, and turkey burgers and tiramisu are so much the 1990s. These are the symbolic dishes, the Jungian culinary icons of their decades. If a dish could be a decade, and a decade could be a dish, this is how things might work out.

When it comes to food, the twentieth century has been a wild and wacky ride across a culinary landscape filled with TV dinners, M&Ms, microwave ovens, granola, Spam, kiwifruit, Tang, Diet Coke, Crock-Pots, electric can openers, pasta machines, Coffee-mate, Caesar salad and tamale pie. We've eaten more different things in this century than all the things eaten in all of recorded history — never before have people had access to the variety of foodstuffs found in a single suburban supermarket. In the annals of food, there's never been anything like the twentieth century. It makes me mighty hungry for what's next — in the twenty-first century.

— Merrill Shindler,
Los Angeles, 1996

How Sweet It Was
1900-1910

It can be argued that the modern age of American cooking began in 1896. As the world quivered with the anticipation of a new century, Fannie Merritt Farmer changed the course of U.S. food history with the publication of her book, *The Boston Cooking School Cookbook*. The director of a teacher training institution, Farmer was the very quintessence of the modern American woman. Her book, a fine cross section of everyday and classic dishes of the time, heralded the use of a precise measuring system in home cookery. Most American home cooking had been, at best, a craft passed on from mother to daughter; Farmer brought rules and science to the kitchen.

Along with providing menus designed mostly for family dinners and luncheons, the educator taught that modern cooks should know what went on in their ovens — and highly controllable gas ovens at that. Eggs did not cook through some magical alchemy; they were cooked because of a chemical reaction caused by heat. She didn't just believe in measurement, she was known as "the mother of level spoonfuls." For Fannie Farmer, a tablespoon was a tablespoon, no more and no less. Cooking properly, for this very proper Bostonian, was an act that ennobled the human race.

But America's appetite for culinary innovation of every sort was seemingly immeasurable. The final years of the nineteenth century and the first decade of the twentieth century may well have been the single most significant period in the culinary history of this country since the discovery of, well, sliced bread.

By the time Fannie Farmer came around, Americans had already become fired up by the culinary teachings of the seer of Battle Creek, John Harvey Kellogg. The Seventh-day Adventist surgeon championed a regimen of vegetarianism, hot baths, exercise, enemas and lots of grains at his famous Health Reform Institute. Kellogg went on to develop scores of cereals before the turn of the century, first with Grunola (later called Granola) and then, rising to the challenge of Shredded Wheat maker H.D. Perky, with the first flaked breakfast cereal. He marketed his Sanitas Corn Flakes with his brother, Will Keith Kellogg. Meanwhile, C.W. Post, a former ulcer patient at Kellogg's Institute, introduced Postum as a healthy alternative to coffee; all this was going on just about the time that an Atlanta druggist, named Dr. John Styth Pemberton, mixed the first batch of Coca-Cola as a remedy for headaches and hangovers in 1886.

By the late 1800s, Jell-O dessert and unsweetened condensed milk were introduced, margarine was made palatable at long last with the addition of palm and arachis oils, peanut butter was invented by a physician in St. Louis as a health-food substitute for dairy butter. Canada Dry ginger ale was born, Thomas Lipton went into the tea business to assure a supply of tea for his chain of grocery stores, the first electric stove was manufactured, the bottle cap was created, and Aunt Jemima Pancake Mix hit the marketplace. Milton Hershey decided to go into the chocolate business. Van Camp's Pork and Beans were introduced, the first pizzeria opened in New York City, the Tootsie Roll was born along with Cracker Jacks, the Campbell Company put out a new product called "Condensed Soup," C.W. Post gave the world Grape-Nuts, National Biscuit Company (or Nabisco, as we know it today) started. The French-German-English dictionary called *Blèuher's Rechtschreibung* announced that in America, people were calling chopped beefsteak "Hamburg steak."

Then the twentieth century began. And it began with a wave of euphoria unlike anything the world had known. Throughout the United States, newspapers declared January 1 the first day of the American Century. Within days, stocks on Wall Street rose so precipitously, a Prosperity Panic was declared. Banker James T. Woodward announced to the press that America was the envy of the entire world.

It was an age of such general affluence that restaurants vied with one another to come up with the most exotic preparation of rare animals and nearly extinct species. Bear was not uncommon in the grand eating rooms of New York, London and Paris. Elk, moose, caribou, elephant, gazelle — all were considered fair game for the palate. There was even a brief flurry of excitement when polar bear steaks were offered at Delmonico's, though it was found soon after that polar bear liver made a poor appetizer — its high level of vitamin A made it toxic enough to kill anyone who ate an order of it with (or without) bacon and onions.

It was also a decade when American sugar consumption soared, hitting sixty-five pounds per person per year. From the British America inherited a national sweet tooth that could not be sated, a fact reflected in the high number of desserts that stand as definitive dishes of the decade, served at both lunch and dinner.

The voracious American appetite began with breakfast. By early 1900, thanks to the Kelloggs, there were forty-two breakfast food plants in Battle Creek, Michigan, each cranking out one or more different brands to satisfy the American need for cereal in the morning. It was a need that severely affected the egg and bacon industries, and they retaliated by mounting advertising campaigns that hinted darkly that breakfast cereal alone wasn't a sufficient meal to help Americans make it through their busy early-twentieth-century day. It worked. Before the decade was over, the standard American breakfast had evolved into a meal of buttered toast, eggs and bacon, and either pancakes or breakfast cereal with milk, a sizable feed that Americans believed was essential — convinced by advertisements informing one and all that breakfast was the most important meal of the day.

In 1900, H.J. Heinz erected what was at the time the largest electric sign in the world — six stories high with twelve hundred light bulbs — announcing that his company offered "57 Good Things for the Table." Wesson Oil was introduced, instantly making cottonseed oil the cooking medium of choice for thousands of modern cooks. In New Haven, Connecticut, a culinary pioneer named Louis Lassen, owner of the three-seat Louis Diner, began serving a sandwich of broiled meat between slices of toasted bread — the very first hamburger. And in San Francisco, the Hills Brothers Company put out the first vacuum-sealed cans of ground roast coffee.

The year 1901 saw the publication of *The Settlement Cook Book*, by the Milwaukee settlement house worker Lizzie Black. Black wrote her book for immigrants to America, to help them learn to cook the American way and to save them the trouble of having to copy recipes off blackboards in classrooms for the foreign born. Her efforts moved the art of cooking even further into the kitchens of common folks.

Barnum's Animal Crackers, Pepsi-Cola and James Drummond Dole's Hawaiian Pineapple Company debuted in 1902 — and so did the first Horn & Hardart Baking Company Automat, in Philadelphia. This was arguably the first fast-food restaurant, a harbinger of the increasing speed of life in these United States and the need Americans would have in the years to come for quick eats — perhaps the defining culinary experience of the second half of the twentieth century.

Before the first decade of the new century was over, the first decaffeinated coffee was perfected and marketed under the name Sanka (a contraction of "sans caffeine"). The ice cream cone was introduced at the 1904 St. Louis World's Fair (by industrious Syrian pastry maker Ernest Hamwi), along with iced tea (by English tea seller Richard Blechynden) to cool the sweltering crowd. Tea bags made their first appearance. So did Campbell's Pork and Beans, French's Mustard, Heinz Baked Beans, Post Toasties, Planter's Peanuts, MSG and frozen strawberries. And the hot dog got its name courtesy of Chicago sports cartoonist Tad Dorgan, who whimsically drew a dachshund inside a bun — the very first hot dog. Within the decade, ice cream sales would skyrocket from five million gallons a year to thirty million gallons. How sweet it was.

It was a decade when Americans felt a national need to satisfy their every urge and to luxuriate in the pride of a country where there was a J. Pierpont Morgan, a John D. Rockefeller, a Henry Ford. Wilbur and Orville Wright had taken the first successful airplane flight. The Panama Canal was under construction, thanks to American know-how and grit. By the end of the decade, the Model T was all the rage. Jack London was the novelist of the day. Blues and jazz were the music to listen to if you were anywhere near the cutting edge. After a century of living in the shadow of Europe, America was the place to be, the forefront of art, culture, science and, for the first time, food.

European chefs, touring America, were astounded by the remarkable quality of the produce and the ability of American industry to turn out products in massive quantities. They also expressed shock at the remarkable amounts of food, especially meat, that Americans consumed at every meal. They came from lands where expensive proteins were stretched with inexpensive starches and vegetables. What they found in America was a bountiful nation where there was no need for filler. Oysters were eaten as an appetizer. Steak was the main course. Salads were generally scorned. Thanks to a canned-goods explosion, anything was available anywhere at any time of the year. Wealth bred indulgence. Being thin was perceived as a sign of failure and penury. Being fat was a mark of affluence and success. Ironically, by the end of the century, those symbols would have completely reversed themselves. But at the century's start, if you were big, life was good. ★

All-American Chocolate Brownies

As increasing numbers of women entered the workforce in the early years of the twentieth century, dishes that could be made in quantity and had a long kitchen life grew in popularity. The first brownie may have been an accident, the result of a forgetful cook neglecting to add baking powder to chocolate cake batter. The first known published recipe for the dense and fudgy dessert appeared in the Sears, Roebuck catalog in 1897 and quickly became a standard in American homes, a dish so popular that a brownie mix was even sold via the catalog. Recipes vary wildly from region to region and from taste to taste; some like their brownies wet and oozing chocolate, while others demand a cakelike dryness.

The basic recipe boils down to:

* **1 cup butter**
* **4 ounces unsweetened chocolate**
* **2 cups sugar**
* **4 eggs**
* **2 teaspoons vanilla**
* **1/2 cup flour**
* **1 cup chopped nuts**

Butter a 9x13-inch baking pan. Melt the chocolate with the butter. Add the remaining ingredients and mix until smooth. Stir in the nuts. Lick the spoon all you want. Pour the batter into the buttered pan. Bake for one hour at 300 degrees.

Makes 16 big brownies

Mom's Apple Pie

There's nothing new or American about apple pie. It dates back to sixteenth-century England and was originally served in this country as a breakfast dish, often with Cheddar cheese. Back at the turn of the century, when life in America was still flavored with innocence, a pie was cooling on every rural windowsill.

Crust

* ★ **2 cups all-purpose flour**
* ★ **2 teaspoons sugar**
* ★ **pinch salt**
* ★ **1/2 cup butter**
* ★ **1/2 cup vegetable shortening**
* ★ **cold water as needed**

Filling

* ★ **2 pounds apples**
* ★ **1 cup sugar**
* ★ **1 teaspoon cinnamon**
* ★ **pinch nutmeg**
* ★ **1/4 cup butter**
* ★ **butter and sugar as needed**

Combine all of the crust ingredients in a large enough container so you don't leave more flour on the floor than in the bowl. Add cold water and mix until the ingredients hold together in a ball. Keep kneading, eventually dividing into two balls. Chill the dough in the fridge.

Heat the oven to 425 degrees. Remove one of the balls from the refrigerator and beat it with a rolling pin until it's the size of a medium pizza. Fit it into a 9-inch pie plate and trim the edges.

Peel, core and thinly slice the apples. Layer on top of the pie crust. Mix together the sugar, cinnamon and nutmeg. Sprinkle over the apples. Break the butter into small bits and scatter on top of the apple and spice filling.

Roll out the second ball of dough. Cover the apple mixture with it. Stick the top crust with a fork for ventilation; this is the time to be artistic. Trim the edges and crimp. Dot the pastry with more butter and sprinkle some sugar on top. Bake for 20 minutes at 425 degrees, and 20 minutes more at 350 degrees. Cool and serve with or without vanilla ice cream.

Serves Six or fewer

Salisbury Steak

This chopped beef dish is one of the more remarkable culinary fads of the fin de
siècle — and the bane to this day of the school cafeteria, where it's often
described in terms unsuited to a general interest cookbook. The recipe was born
with Dr. James Henry Salisbury, a British physician who believed that extremely
lean chopped beef was the be-all and end-all of cures for what ails you. He rec-
ommended that the meat, always cooked until it was well done, should be eaten
three times a day and that a glass of hot water should be drunk before and after.
The good doctor's research told him that this regimen would cure tuberculosis,
gout, asthma, rheumatism, colitis and anemia. It was, and still is, basically a
hamburger without a bun — and without much taste either. The original was
absurdly bland but it caught on in America, where Salisbury had many followers.
Later versions have improved it considerably.

---

* ★ **cooking oil**
* ★ **1/2 cup chopped onions**
* ★ **2 pounds chopped beef**
* ★ **1 cup bread crumbs**
* ★ **salt and pepper**

Saute the onions in oil until they're tender. Combine them with the beef, bread crumbs, salt and pepper and divide into six thick patties. Cook until the meat is more than rare, less than well done, then turn and cook on the flip side. Serve with steamed vegetables, without ketchup, without mustard, without mayonnaise, without a bun, without relish.

Serves Six

Baked Alaska

Though this classic dessert dates back to the heady days following the purchase of Alaska from Russia in 1867, it became one of the defining dishes of the golden age of the 1890s and 1900s, a rather overdone dish that smacked of high exoticism, railroad barons and meals concluded with snifters of cognac. Many an aspiring cook tried to impress guests with baked Alaska, only to be faced with a molten mess. There are reasons that baked Alaska lives today more as a memory than as a dish worth struggling through.

---

* **1 loaf-shaped sponge cake or pound cake**
* **1 quart vanilla ice cream**
* **6 egg whites**
* **2 teaspoons vanilla**
* **pinch cream of tartar**
* **1/2 cup sugar**
* **9 halved marshmallows**

Preheat oven to 450 degrees. Place the cake on an ovenproof plate. Cover the cake on top and sides using all the ice cream and store it in the freezer while you make a meringue. Beat the egg whites, vanilla, cream of tartar and sugar until stiff peaks form. Cover the ice cream and cake with the meringue (the thick meringue will keep the heat from melting the ice cream, but you must watch it carefully to avoid a creamy disaster). Top with the marshmallow halves. Bake in the hot oven for about two to four minutes or until the meringue is light brown. Serve before the ice cream melts. Good luck.

Serves Six to Eight

Club Sandwich

In this, the decade of men's clubs, one of the great American sandwiches was born. It has been claimed over the years by nearly every men's club in New York, but the Saratoga Club in Saratoga, New York, is most often credited.

It is a sandwich about which there's much disagreement. Though it's usually presented as a double-decker production with three slices of bread, culinary historians argue that the original club was just a single decker. Variations on the theme have abounded through the years – the 1964 edition of Joy of Cooking *suggests adding drained slices of pineapple, which seems awfully effete. One of the pleasures of the club sandwich is how unabashedly manly the whole construction tends to be.*

---

* **3 slices toasted bread (white is preferred)**
* **freshly cooked bacon**
* **cold boneless chicken breast**
* **sliced tomato**
* **lettuce leaves**
* **lots of mayonnaise**

Build a chicken, bacon, lettuce, tomato and mayonnaise sandwich. Then build a second sandwich atop the first. Be unashamed in your use of mayonnaise. Use a toothpick to hold the whole thing together. Top with a black or green olive or a pickle slice.

Serves One

Deviled Eggs

Dishes have been bedeviled for the past several centuries. But it was around the turn of the century that deviled eggs became a nationwide craze, appearing in a myriad of novels of the time and often mentioned — along with fried chicken — as the quintessential picnic dish. To this day there's a primal taste found in a deviled egg, which for some people is the most palatable thing ever done to eggs. And one of the easiest.

---

* **6 hard-cooked eggs**
* **3 tablespoons chopped pickle**
* **1 teaspoon prepared mustard (the less fancy, the better)**
* **1/4 cup mayonnaise**
* **salt and pepper**
* **paprika**

Peel the eggs and slice them lengthwise, carefully removing the yolks. Mash the yolks together with the pickle, mustard, mayonnaise, salt and pepper (white pepper works especially well). Carefully refill the egg whites with the yolk mixture. Sprinkle with paprika.

Serves Two

Devil's Food Cake

Devil's food cake was one of the great fad desserts of the first decade of the century, a dish that appeared on menus at every level of society. The rich gave it fancy names like Devil's Food Cockaigne. For the rest of us, we had our cake . . . and we ate it too. Devil's food cake seemed so much more appealing than angel's food cake. It may be because of America's deep-seated affection for chocolate, which has often bordered on the obsessive.

Cake

* ★ 3/4 cup butter
* ★ 1 cup brown sugar
* ★ 3 eggs, well beaten
* ★ 3 squares unsweetened chocolate
* ★ 2-1/2 cups cake flour
* ★ 1-1/2 teaspoons double-acting baking powder
* ★ pinch salt
* ★ 3/4 cup milk
* ★ 1-1/2 teaspoons vanilla

Frosting

* ★ 3 cups confectioners sugar
* ★ 6 tablespoons butter
* ★ 1/4 cup cream
* ★ 1 teaspoon vanilla extract
* ★ 2 teaspoons corn syrup
* ★ 4 one-ounce bars bittersweet chocolate

Melt the butter and add the sugar, stirring until smooth. Slowly add the beaten eggs. Melt the chocolate until it's smooth and thick; cool and mix with the eggs. Add the flour, baking powder, salt, milk and vanilla. Beat until smooth. Pour into a buttered 9x13-inch pan. Bake at 350 degrees for 30 minutes. Check for doneness by inserting a thin stainless steel knife. When it comes out clean, the cake should be done.

To make the frosting, mix the sugar with the butter until creamy. Add the cream, vanilla and syrup, blending constantly. Melt chocolate, cool, blend into frosting. Makes two and one-half cups.

When the cake is cool, ice it. Or, if you're in a hurry, use canned chocolate frosting, which tastes almost as good as the real thing and saves a lot of trouble.

Serves Eight

Muffaletta Sandwich

At the same time that the club sandwich was all the rage in much of America, Cajun and Creole cooking styles fused with the tastes of a steadily increasing Italian population in New Orleans to create one of the most daunting of all American sandwiches, a Brobdingnagian massivity called the Muffaletta, whose roots trace to the city's fabled Central Grocery. It's a sandwich that can still be found in the Crescent City, where it fits well with the "always for pleasure" attitude of America's most culinarily obsessed metropolis. This is a sandwich that can't possibly be eaten with anything even vaguely resembling finesse. One bite, and it's all over you. It's built that way.

---

* **1 round Italian bread loaf, heavy with sesame seeds**
* **lots of ham**
* **lots of salami**
* **lots of cheese**
* **Italian pickled vegetable salad**
* **olive oil to taste**

The idea is to create a sandwich that's literally too big to eat. Slice the bread loaf in half, creating a top and a bottom. Pull out all the interior dough you can. Fill it with slices of ham, salami (several types work nicely, especially Genoa and mortadella) and various cheeses (choose from provolone, mozzarella, Monterey jack, Swiss, cheddar). Then top with the pickled vegetable salad. You can make this salad, which is a simple olive condiment made of green, Greek and black olives, cauliflower, celery, parsley, oregano, pimento and garlic, all marinated in a blend of one-part olive oil to two-parts vinegar. Ladies at the turn of the century often bought theirs at the Central Grocery. Today you can opt to buy Progresso's very good version. Whichever you choose, toss in extra olives if you like and pour on some olive oil if you dare. Then bite in.

Feeds four normal people or one New Orleans resident

Oysters Rockefeller

Along with the Cobb salad and the Caesar salad, this was one of the most famous of all American dishes of the twentieth century. It was invented by Jules Alciatore of Antoine's in New Orleans in 1899 as a way of dealing with a shortage of French snails. It was named for John D. Rockefeller not because he was a regular customer but simply because he was the richest man in the nation, which seemed to match the richness of the dish. (These days, it would be called oysters Bill Gates, which somehow lacks the same panache.) Though most people believe this dish is made with spinach (and most recipes agree with that contention), the owners of Antoine's have long denied the presence of spinach in their version — and hold the recipe a closely guarded secret. The original was most likely topped with a mixture of chervil, tarragon, celery and scallions. But oysters and spinach are one of those marriages of taste made in heaven . . .

---

* **2 dozen raw oysters on the half shell**
* **4 slices raw bacon**
* **1 cup cooked spinach**
* **4 teaspoons chopped parsley**
* **2 scallions**
* **1/2 teaspoon salt**
* **pinch cayenne pepper**
* **pinch paprika**
* **1/4 cup grated Parmesan**
* **4 tablespoons melted butter**
* **3 tablespoons lemon juice**
* **2 tablespoons bread crumbs**
* **rock salt as needed**

Place the oysters on a bed of rock salt and broil slowly until they begin to curl at the edges. Chop together the bacon, spinach, parsley and scallions (a food processor is the best way to do that). Place in a pot, add the remaining ingredients and bring to a boil. Spoon some sauce over each oyster. Return to the broiler and brown lightly.

Serves Four

Pineapple Upside-down Cake

In the first decades of this century, there was hardly a ladies magazine in America
that didn't include a recipe for one sort of upside-down cake or another. This fad
that reached its apex in the thirties began simply in the early 1900s with a cake
that was more often than not cooked in an iron skillet, then topped and flipped
— a bit like a pancake turned into a cake. In time it evolved into the ultimate
bridge-party treat, a dish whose very making defined the culinary skill of the lady
who attempted it.

Cake

* ★ 2 cups all-purpose flour
* ★ 1 cup sugar
* ★ 1 tablespoon double-acting
  baking powder
* ★ pinch salt
* ★ 3/4 cup butter
* ★ 1 cup milk
* ★ 2 teaspoons vanilla
* ★ 2 large eggs

Topping

* ★ 6 tablespoons butter
* ★ 1-1/2 cups brown sugar
* ★ 12 drained pineapple rings
* ★ 12 halved maraschino cherries

Combine the flour, sugar, baking powder and salt. Add softened butter, milk and vanilla. Mix till well blended. Add the eggs, beat very well. Grease a 9x13-inch baking pan.

Melt the butter for topping. Add the sugar and mix well. Pour into the bottom of the greased pan. Arrange pineapple rings and cherries cut in half. Pour in the cake batter. Bake at 350 degrees for 40 minutes. Invert the cake on a plate, and cool before serving.

Serves Twelve

The Melting Pot Bubbles Over
1910~1920

In retrospect, the decade of the 1910s is so totally dominated by World War I (or, as it was known at the time, the Great War) that we tend to forget that, for the United States at least, the war only lasted from April 6, 1917, to November 11, 1918. As American involvements go, it was brief and to the point. For the British and the French, World War I was an endless horror. For America, the war was basically a police action that happened "over there." True, riots over food shortages broke out in New York, wheat and food prices rose, and sugar rationing was ordered. War posters admonished Americans not to waste food while others starved.

In culinary terms, the second decade of the century was notable, in broad strokes, as the era during which vitamins were classified (in 1911), and dietary studies on their importance became one of the themes of the age. In the same way that we obsess over HDL, LDL and triglycerides today, in the 1910s all the talk was of the importance of vitamins A, the various Bs, C, D and E. There was much controversy about whether sufficient vitamins could be obtained from everyday food or whether supplements were needed to maintain proper health. Ninety years later, nothing has changed; those who gobble vitamins by the handful are convinced that no amount of fresh broccoli will suffice.

It was in 1912 that cellophane was first produced. It would in time do wonders for the world of food preparation and preservation (can you imagine not covering your leftovers with Saran Wrap?). Pyrex came along in 1915. And there was a steady shift in the way that Americans ate their meals. In 1890, 80 percent of all the bread consumed in the United States was baked at home. By 1910 that number had dropped to 70 percent. (By 1924 it had plummeted to 30 percent as Americans decided that bakers should bake breads in bakeries, ending a tradition that had virtually defined American cooking since the first settlers.)

By 1910 Aunt Jemima had turned into a national icon. Thanks to some dazzlingly brilliant marketing, pancakes — which had long been considered a cold-weather dish — were repositioned as a breakfast item to enjoy all year long. Americans continued to believe that breakfasts should be big. However, rather than consuming cold meats and cheese for breakfast, as had long been the habit in many parts of the country, bread, pancakes and cereals were all the rage — arguably a proper cuisine for a nation that was becoming steadily far more urban and far less rural. Country work demands sustenance; city work more often than not simply requires filler. There were 108 brands of corn flakes pouring out of Battle Creek, Michigan, with Kellogg's and Post

Toasties well ahead of the competition.

The early 1910s were also a time of immigration unequaled in American history. On April 17, 1911, for example, 11, 745 immigrants passed through New York's Ellis Island — more than had ever arrived on one day before and more than have ever arrived on any day since. Those immigrants brought along their lunch — and their dinner. Before the decade was over, the ghettos of New York, Boston, Chicago and Philadelphia would be redolent with the smells of Jewish, Italian, Polish, German, Chinese, Russian, Czech and Romanian cooking. Since cuisine is never static, the melting pot was brought to a high boil. It wasn't long before individual dishes began to make their way into the mildly Gallic, largely British style of cooking that passed for cuisine in the United States. Hyphens began to appear everywhere — Italian-American, Chinese-American, German-American, Jewish-American.

The cooking, as a rule, was a bit of this and a bit of that. It was accepted a lot more readily than the immigrants who brought it with them. Human bias was everywhere, but culinary bias was sporadic at worst, nonexistent at best. And if it was made in the U. S., even if it was "foreign" food, it had to be cleaner, figured at least one food critic of the time. At the start of the decade, virtually all of the pasta eaten in the United States was imported from Italy. By the end of the decade, most pasta was produced in America — a trend certainly helped along by the war in Europe.

The search for gustatory pleasures became an upper-class pastime for people who delighted in knowing where to find and how to order the best special dishes at unexpected ethnic restaurants. "When one exclaims in ecstasy over a wonderful flavor found in some dingy restaurant, let him not be surprised if he learns that the chef who concocted the dish boasts royal decoration for tickling the palate of some epicurean ruler of a foreign land," wrote Clarence E. Edwords, a self-labeled bohemian in San Francisco in 1914. Ethnic restaurants, he noted, "can secure the delicacies imported by these foreign storekeepers to supply the wants of their people."

A table d'hôte dinner at a good restaurant was a several course affair, from cantaloupe, consommé, potage or cherrystone clams to cassoulet of lobster, sauteed sweetbreads, spaghetti with a Menagére sauce, supréme of chicken, pâté de maison or steak, salad, cheese and sweets. In the early part of the century, remedies for the chronically underweight surpassed those for the morbidly overweight. However, some people were beginning to wonder if Americans weren't getting a little too big for their breeches and whether all that eating was really healthy. In 1911, the fasting cure, promulgated by Upton Sinclair in his book of the same name, enjoyed popularity among some health faddists, especially in California where Sinclair was then living.

In 1912, a German-American delicatessen owner named Richard Hellman came up with Hellman's Blue Ribbon Mayonnaise (known today as Best Foods Mayonnaise on the western side of the country). That same year National Biscuit Company, which wouldn't use the name Nabisco until 1941, introduced a cookie it called the Oreo Biscuit (in the fifties, the name was changed to the Oreo Cream Sandwich, but to most of us, these cookies are just Oreos). Quaker Puffed Wheat and Quaker Puffed Rice came on the scene in 1913, along with Peppermint Life Savers. Kraft Processed Cheese was born in 1915. Nathan's Famous Frankfurters were introduced in 1916 by Polish-American Nathan Handwerker at a stand on New York's Coney Island. Inventor Charles Strite took out a patent on the first automatic pop-up toaster. Los Angeles noodle manufacturer David Jung invented the fortune cookie, soon a staple at most Chinese restaurants. National ice cream consumption rose from thirty million gallons in 1909 to one hundred-fifty million gallons in 1919.

The decade was also host to three of the most important changes in American cuisine to strike the nation. In 1914, a New York fur trader named Clarence Birdseye, while on a trip to Labrador, noticed that fish caught in the dead of winter froze rock hard almost as soon as they were exposed to the frigid air. He further noticed that when they were defrosted and cooked weeks and even months later, they tasted almost as good as they had when fresh. It was a phenomenon, long known by those who lived in colder climes, that he began to look into. In 1917, he returned to New York with a clear understanding of the process of fast freezing and the further discovery that

cabbages frozen in seawater could be restored to life without an unreasonable loss of taste. By the late twenties, this would eventually change the course of American eating.

Perhaps an even more profound change resulted from the birth of the self-service market, a highly radical idea that popped up in various parts of the country at pretty much the same time. The title of first self-service grocery is claimed by the Alpha Beta Food Markets (whose name came from the simple device of arranging the goods on the shelves in alphabetical order) of Pomona, California; Ward's Groceteria of Ocean Park, California; and Piggly Wiggly of Memphis, Tennessee. Prior to this time, the customers were served by clerks. If it was a pound of potatoes they needed, the clerk would package it for them. If it was a can of beans they needed, the clerk would collect that as well. At the end of your shopping, it would all be wrapped up in kraft paper and delivered to your door or perhaps loaded into your wagon.

By removing the barrier between the customer and the food, the entire dynamic of culinary interchange was rearranged. Consumers could touch the bananas, fondle the melons, caress the chickens. Rather than being at the mercy of the clerks, they were seemingly in charge. It was a revolution in quality and, for that matter, in availability and efficiency.

The third change came at the very end of the decade. Until then, cocktails and champagne flowed freely through dinners at upscale and cosmopolitan restaurants. In January 1919, the Eighteenth Amendment to the Constitution of the United States was ratified, to go into effect on January 16, 1920. It prohibited the sale of alcoholic beverages anywhere in the United States. Along with it went the Prohibition Enforcement Act, also known as the Volstead Act, which defined any beverage containing more than one half of one percent alcohol to be intoxicating. As has often been pointed out, orange juice often has that much alcohol. The Great Experiment had begun. It would, in the decade that followed, make America thirstier than ever. ★

The Daiquiri

In the years following the Spanish-American War, Americans became increasingly obsessed with Cuba and the Caribbean in general, one of the primary tourist destinations of the time. The Caribbean was perceived as the South Pacific without all the inconveniences. And the love of things tropical inspired a rum frenzy, capped by a nationwide craze for a drink from Cuba called the Daiquiri (apparently named for the Cuban town of Daiquiri, a rather rough mining settlement). The frozen Daiquiri came along years later, along with the pink Daiquiri. The original was eminently low maintenance.

* **1 tablespoon lime juice**
* **1 tablespoon sugar syrup**
  (or 1 teaspoon superfine sugar)
* **2-1/2 ounces light Jamaican rum**

Pour all ingredients into a shaker with ice. Shake vigorously. Strain into a Martini glass. Drink slowly; Daiquiris tend to go straight to your head.

Serves One

Chicken à la King

Though chicken à la king is almost certainly a dish of the nineteenth century, with a birthright claimed by restaurants as varied as New York's Brighton Beach Hotel, the fabled Delmonico's and Claridge's in London, it wasn't until the twentieth century that it became a deep-seated American standard. It had even spawned a variation by the 1910s, called salmon à la king, that was especially popular in the Midwest. If a Minnesota housewife wanted to impress guests, she served salmon à la king. The same recipe works just fine for both chicken and salmon.

---

* **2 tablespoons butter**
* **1 minced green pepper**
* **1 minced onion**
* **1 cup sliced mushrooms**
* **2 tablespoons flour**
* **1 cup chicken stock**
* **2 cups diced cooked chicken (or)**
* **2 cups canned red salmon**
* **1 cup light cream**
* **2 egg yolks**
* **1 teaspoon diced pimiento**
* **salt and pepper**
* **4 teaspoons sherry**
* **toast triangles**

Melt the butter and saute the green pepper, onion and mushrooms in it. Remove and save the veggies. Stir in the flour. Add the stock and cook until thick, stirring constantly. Add the chicken or salmon, along with the vegetables. Mix the cream with the egg yolks, spoon some sauce into the cream and egg yolk mixture, and whisk well. Add the cream and egg yolk mixture to the chicken and stir in well. Season with pimiento, salt and pepper and sherry, and then ladle over toast.

Serves Four

Chop Suey

The oft-maligned chop suey is genuine Chinese-American cuisine, the cooking style that grew out of the efforts of laborers from Canton to re-create their wives' cooking. Thanks to the Chinese exclusion laws of the late nineteenth century, many of these railroad and mine workers were unable to send for the families they had left in China. Since the men had never been the family cooks, their memories of the food were confused at best. When they combined their recollections with the American cooking they encountered every day, the result was one of the great fad cuisines of the 1910s. The best-known Chinese-American dish was, of course, chop suey. Most popular of all was chicken chop suey.

* **1 three-pound chicken**
* **water as needed**
* **1/2 cup peanut oil**
* **3 stalks celery, sliced**
* **12 roughly chopped water chestnuts**
* **1 cup chicken stock**
* **4 tablespoons soy sauce**
* **1/2 pound bean sprouts**
* **12 white mushrooms, sliced**
* **1 tablespoon cornstarch**

Boil the chicken until it's done. Discard the skin and bones. Shred the meat. In a wok, heat the peanut oil, add the chicken and cook lightly. Add the celery, water chestnuts and stock. Cook for ten minutes, stirring often. Add the soy sauce, bean sprouts and mushrooms, trying not to overcook them. Mix cornstarch with a little cold water, let sit for a few moments to settle, then stir again to dissolve cornstarch. Add to chop suey and simmer for three to four minutes. Serve hot with white rice.

Serves Eight

Chow Mein

This is a bit more authentically Chinese than chop suey. The name comes from the Mandarin term meaning "fried noodles," and it's a dish that straddles the boundary between Chinese cooking and Chinese-American cooking. It's often found on the menus of the genuine Chinese restaurants of New York, San Francisco and Los Angeles. Back in the 1910s, chow mein, along with chop suey (and egg foo young, sub gum chicken and egg drop soup), was part of the pantheon of the "choose one from column A and two from column B" school of Chinese menus. Though chicken chow mein is a standard, barbecued pork chow mein comes closest to the original.

---

* **1 pound egg noodles**

  water as needed

* **1/2 cup peanut oil**

* **3 onions, cut into eighths**

* **2 cups sliced celery**

* **1 tablespoon water**

* **2 cups sliced bok choy**

* **3 cups sliced barbecued pork (pur chased from an Asian market if possible)**

* **2 tablespoons bottled oyster sauce**

* **3 tablespoons soy sauce**

* **1 tablespoon cornstarch**

* **1 cup chicken stock**

* **1/2 pound bean sprouts**

* **1 bunch scallions, cut into one-inch pieces**

* **1 teaspoon sugar**

Boil the noodles till done but still firm, then drain well. Place them on an oiled cookie sheet and bake at 350 degrees for 25 minutes. Flip the noodles over and bake for 15 more minutes. While the noodles cool, prepare the vegetables.

Heat the peanut oil in a wok. First cook the onions and celery in oil for two minutes, then add the tablespoon of water and cook for a minute more. Add the bok choy and cook for one more minute. Add the roast pork and sauces. Add the noodles, broken into small pieces. Make a sauce by combining the cornstarch and chicken stock. Add the remaining ingredients, and stir-fry over high heat. Try not to overcook the stuff — and don't serve it with rice; noodles and rice are a silly idea.

Serves Six

The Ramos Gin Fizz

In the heady years leading into the Roaring Twenties, this drink, which goes down with unabashed ease and leaves the consumer incapable of mobility after more than one, was the drink of choice in polite society, especially as a Sunday morning libation (a position it assumed again in the seventies and eighties). Henry C. Ramos, the New Orleans barkeep, supposedly invented it as a way of coping with the hangovers of the night before.

---

* ★ **1 teaspoon confectioners sugar**
* ★ **1 ounce lemon juice**
* ★ **1 ounce cream**
* ★ **1-1/2 ounces gin**
* ★ **3 dashes orange-flower water**
* ★ **1 egg white**

Shake all ingredients well with ice until foamy or whip in a blender. Serve in a chilled iced-tea glass.

Serves One

Key Lime Pie

Along with the national obsession with things Caribbean came a love of things Floridian and, in particular, the Florida Keys — land of the alligator, the pompano and the increasingly rare Key lime. Smaller, rounder and yellower than other limes, the intensely flavorful fruit was used to make Key lime pie as early as the mid-1800s. By the 1910s no proper restaurant was without its version, often made with whatever limes the cooks could get their hands on.

Crust

* ★ 2 cups graham cracker crumbs
* ★ 1/2 cup sugar
* ★ 1 teaspoon cinnamon
* ★ 1/2 cup melted butter

Filling

* ★ 1 large can Eagle Brand sweetened condensed milk
* ★ 3/4 cup Key lime juice (or bottled lime juice if Key lime juice isn't available)
* ★ 6 egg yolks
* ★ 3/4 cup heavy cream
* ★ 2 tablespoons sugar
* ★ 1/2 teaspoon vanilla extract

Combine the first four ingredients and mix together till moist and mushy. Pour into a 9-inch pie pan and smooth out as much as possible. Bake at 350 degrees for ten minutes, then cool.

Beat the condensed milk, lime juice and egg yolks until the mixture begins to look like pudding. Pour into the baked pie shell and bake at 300 degrees for 20 minutes or until it's set. Then refrigerate and forget about it for at least three hours.

Later on, beat the cream, sugar and vanilla until the mixture begins to stiffen. Take the pie out of the fridge, spread the cream on top, and step out of the way.

Serves Six

Palace Court Salad

Also known as Palm Court Salad, Garden Court Salad, San Francisco Salad and Bay Artichoke Salad, among many other variations, it was one of the prime salads in an age when greens were viewed with something akin to suspicion. During its heyday, it was a rare upper-crust meal that didn't include some variation on this simple combination of artichokes with a mayonnaise and crabmeat topping.

---

* **shredded lettuce**
* **sliced tomatoes**
* **3 artichoke bottoms, marinated or unmarinated**
* **1 tablespoon minced scallions**
* **1/4 cup cooked crabmeat**
* **1/4 cup mayonnaise**
* **garnishes of your choice**

Layer artichoke hearts and tomatoes on a bed of lettuce. Combine the scallions with crabmeat and mayonnaise (in some versions, celery is used instead of scallions), and top the tomatoes and artichoke hearts with the mixture. Garnish with black olives, slices of hard-cooked egg, cooked vegetables …whatever comes to mind.

Serves Two

Red Flannel Hash

Probably the best known working-class dish of the early years of the century, red flannel hash was the great catchall for leftovers, especially those from the popular and populist feast called the boiled dinner, a sizable pot of corned beef cooked with beets (hence the redness), carrots, onions, potatoes, beans, cabbage, brown sugar and maple syrup — a combination of entree and dessert on one plate. It came to mean almost any sort of leftover hash. You'll notice there are no amounts listed for the ingredients. The essence of red flannel hash is that there are none. It's a dish made purely of leftovers, and cooks threw everything they had into the pan and cooked them up. That's the pleasure of this dish. When hash became a necessity during the Depression, it achieved something akin to lower-class gourmet status; it meant there was dinner that night.

---

* **leftover meat (preferably corned beef)**
* **leftover vegetables (especially potatoes and, if possible, beets)**
* **bacon or salt pork**
* **eggs**

Combine the meat, bread crumbs, milk, eggs, onions, parsley, herbs and spices by hand until smooth. Form into meatballs. Melt the butter in a large skillet, and cook the meat-balls until they're brown all over. Store in a warm oven while you make the gravy.

Add the two tablespoons of butter to the drippings in the skillet, stir in the flour, blend well and brown. Add the mustards and stock, and stir until smooth and bubbly. Add the meatballs, and cook until they're well coated with gravy. Traditionally served over egg noodles.

Serves however many you want to serve

Swedish Meatballs

As the Scandinavian population of the Midwest grew, a Swedish cooking mini-trend spread to Chicago and New York, where massive smorgasbords became quite the thing. Though herring was looked on with some disdain (its deep ethnic roots made it seem a bit too low-rent for proper folks), Swedish meatballs appeared on menus in every manner of restaurant. They also became a staple for appetizers served at home, perhaps the first time in American history that meatballs became haute cuisine.

Meatballs

* ★ 1 pound ground beef (or a combination of beef, pork and veal)
* ★ 1 cup stale white bread crumbs
* ★ 1/2 cup milk
* ★ 2 eggs
* ★ 1/2 cup chopped onions
* ★ 1/4 cup chopped parsley
* ★ pinch allspice
* ★ 1/2 teaspoon paprika
* ★ 1/2 teaspoon dill weed
* ★ butter for frying

Gravy

* ★ 2 tablespoons butter
* ★ 2 tablespoons unbleached flour
* ★ 1 teaspoon Colman's mustard
* ★ 1 teaspoon Dijon mustard
* ★ 2 cups chicken stock

Combine the meat, bread crumbs, milk, eggs, onions, parsley, herbs and spices by hand until smooth. Form into meatballs. Melt the butter in a large skillet, and cook the meatballs until they're brown all over. Store in a warm oven while you make the gravy.

Add the two tablespoons of butter to the drippings in the skillet, stir in the flour, blend well and brown. Add the mustards and stock, and stir until smooth and bubbly. Add the meatballs, and cook until they're well coated with gravy. Traditionally served over egg noodles.

Serves Six

Vichyssoise

What may well be the most famous gourmet soup of the twentieth century, a dish with a quintessentially French name, is wholly unknown in France (or at least was, until American hotel chains began putting it on menus there). Vichyssoise is credited to Chef Louis Diat of the Ritz-Carlton in New York sometime in the 1910s. By the end of the decade it was accepted as the proper soup for any serious gathering of affluent citizens, a position it retained throughout the century. As far as the name goes, the apocryphal story has the chef not only concocting a refreshing soup for warm days, but also the most Gallic name he could come up with. He did a fine job on both accounts.

---

* **4 tablespoons butter**
* **4 leeks, the white part only, carefully washed to remove any sand**
* **1 well-chopped medium onion**
* **3 well-chopped medium potatoes**
* **4 cups chicken stock**
* **salt and pepper**
* **1/2 teaspoon nutmeg**
* **1 bay leaf**
* **2 cups cream**
* **1 tablespoon chopped chives**

In a pot, melt butter, add chopped leeks and potatoes, and saute until soft. Remove from pot, and saute onions in remaining butter. Return vegetables to pot and add chicken stock, salt and pepper to taste, then the nutmeg and bay leaf. Cook over low heat for 30 minutes. Remove the bay leaf and put soup into blender (Chef Diat probably pressed his through a strainer, but why would we bother today?). Blend until smooth. Strain the soup into a large bowl and cool. Gently stir in the cream and pour into individual soup bowls (over ice if possible), and garnish with chives.

Serves Four

The Salad Years
1920~1930

The restrictions of Prohibition notwithstanding, the twenties (I dislike the term the Roaring Twenties, but it must be mentioned) was a decade of remarkable affluence and unprecedented discretionary income. Though the stock market boom of the decade would turn out to be illusory, it did cause people to think there was lots of money to be made and lots to be spent. And spend it Americans did, on fine dining in the big cities, in hotel dining rooms, in grand clubs, in glamorous bistros and boîtes.

One of the defining images of the decade is of the swells, dressed to the nines, dancing the Charleston and the Black Bottom at the opulent clubs of New York and of a new up-and-coming film community called Hollywood, where folks had more money than they could imagine what to do with. Thanks to Hollywood, America also got a bee in its collective bonnet about the right body shape. After years of stoutness being viewed as a sign of prosperity and success, the slim profile came into vogue. And along with the need to drop a little avoirdupois came the rise of the salad.

Until now, Americans had viewed vegetables in general with little enthusiasm. Salads had a long history as a strictly aristocratic dish and thus were scorned by the populace, which thought those delicate little leaves were kind of silly. In the late 1800s, however, leafy greens were adopted by very rich Americans in an effort to ape the dining habits of the European upper crust. In the early 1900s, the habit of eating salads with meals began to trickle down from the very rich to the rich to the middle class to the hoi polloi.

By the 1920s, it was the rare family that didn't sit down to a green salad before their evening meal. Once Hollywood put its imprimatur on dressed greens, with the creation of the Cobb salad at the Brown Derby and the adoption of Caesar Cardini's Tijuana-born Caesar salad, they became not just side dishes but main courses as well. In terms of the twentieth century, the 1920s were our salad years.

Not all Americans were into salads. In fact, soft drink and ice cream sales boomed. The American sweet tooth, deprived of the sugar content of alcohol, cried out for candy. American industry did what it could to satisfy that need. The chocolate-covered Good Humor bar was born in Youngstown, Ohio. The Baby Ruth was introduced, named not for Babe Ruth (as most people assume to this day) but for Baby Ruth Cleveland, daughter of President Grover Cleveland. The Oh Henry bar was born in Chicago, along with Jujyfruits, the automatic doughnut-making machine, the Mounds bar, the

Milky Way bar, the Butterfinger bar, Hostess Cakes and 7-Up.

Other important developments were also brewing. In the 1890s, twice as many households in America had domestic servants as had them in the 1920s, a remarkable change in the way that America took care of its daily domestic work. The effect on American cuisine was extreme — what evolved was a new world of "labor-saving devices" that helped housewives take care of their chores in nothing flat. These devices included every manner of kitchen gadget imaginable. Where much had been done by hand (as in the case of baking bread), now much was either done by machine or simply purchased at the market. If the middle class had to do it themselves, they were going to take as many shortcuts as possible. Efficiency became the byword of the age. Unfortunately, flavor and quality often suffered in the process.

Technically speaking, Americans were supposed to have stopped drinking alcoholic beverages on January 16, 1920. In actuality, they stopped drinking only long enough to set up basement and backyard stills, wineries and breweries. A massive business developed almost overnight, selling solid citizens the implements needed for establishing an underground operation that would keep wine and beer flowing. Yeast and hop sales boomed, bottles became a scarce commodity, corks all but disappeared from the marketplace. Bathtub gin wasn't just a witty name. It was a reality.

Those who could afford it bought the smuggled liquor that virtually flooded over the borders; at times, the coast of Florida and the border with Canada seemed more like open-air spirits shops than lines of demarcation. It's been estimated that by the middle of the decade, more alcoholic beverages were actually entering the country than had been sold in America prior to Prohibition. In other words, Prohibition not only didn't diminish drinking, it may very well have increased it. Human nature is such that people want what they can't have. And what Americans couldn't have was beer and wine, whiskey and rye, bourbon and Scotch.

Prohibition's effects on our habits were occasionally direct — as in the immediate disappearance of the grand tradition of the free lunch, which had been served at bars and saloons in every major metropolis. Actually, the free lunch was rarely free; barkeepers felt that a small fee was necessary to keep the riffraff out, giving us the timeless aphorism that there's no such thing as a free lunch. During Prohibition, there was definitely no such thing as a free lunch, for there were no bars and saloons in which to serve it.

The result was the great age of the diner. Legions of displaced barkeeps recognized that even if they couldn't serve alcoholic beverages (at least, not above the counter), their customers still needed a place to go for an inexpensive breakfast, lunch or dinner. Though the railroad-car diner had existed before 1920, it went through a resurgence at the start of Prohibition that gave us literally hundreds of places to go for a plate o' beef and a cup o' joe. Some remarkable spots are still around to this day — the Apple Tree Diner in Dedham, Massachusetts; the Hi-Way Diner in New Haven, Connecticut; the Seagull Diner in Kittery, Maine; the Big E Diner in Closter, New Jersey; the Blue Dolphin Diner in Katonah, New York.

They were, and are, fine places to find the meat 'n' taters cooking that's come to be recognized as American cuisine. They also gave us a wealth of colorful phrases that have become culinary colloquialisms: Adam and Eve on a raft (poached eggs on toast), Adam and Eve on a raft and wreck 'em (break the yolks), dress 'em up (make it to go), eighty-six (throw the customer out), eighty-one (glass of water) eighty-seven (good-looking customer), java and joe (coffee), stretch it (make it large), squeeze one (orange juice), fish eggs (tapioca pudding), sweep up the kitchen for one (hash), fried cake (doughnuts), Popeye (spinach), two lookin' at ya (eggs, sunnyside up), two to trot (two coffees to go), bowwow (hot dog), belch water (seltzer), burn the Brits (toasted English muffin), bowl of red (chili con carne), Eve with a lid on (apple pie), Mike and Ike (salt and pepper) and more, many more. For the great mass of Americans, the diner — a.k.a. the lunch counter, the lunch wagon, the crumb hall, the short-order joint, the hash house, the slop house, the ham and eggery, the beanery, the bean wagon, the dog wagon, the greasy spoon, the hash foundry, the chew and choke, and the quick and dirty — was the closest they'd come to the experience of dining out. Prior to the advent of Mickey D's, the diner was the great American restaurant, serving the great American cuisine.

Henry Ford introduced barbecue grilling as we know it to this country when, in the 1920s, to encourage people to go on picnics, he marketed little portable barbecues. Not one to waste anything he could sell, Ford used the sawdust and wood scraps left over from making Model T's to manufacture compressed charcoal briquettes. It was also the decade that gave us Land o' Lakes Butter, Wheaties, Hormel Flavor-Sealed Ham, Wonder Bread, Lender's Bagels, Gerber Baby Foods, the Marriott Hot Shoppe, Peter Pan Peanut Butter, Rice Krispies, General Mills, Wise Potato Chips, General Foods, Standard Brands . . . and Betty Crocker. Betty would go on to become a culinary icon of the twentieth century — even though she was the creation of the marketing department of the Washburn Crosby Company of Minneapolis — a "food expert" born to help promote their new Gold Medal Flour. Her birth in the twenties was perfect, for it was a decade filled with illusions and wealth built out of smoke and mirrors. By 1929, though Betty Crocker persevered, the smoke was gone and the mirrors had all cracked. ★

Caesar Salad

What would eventually become the sine qua non of American salads was born one hot, dusty Fourth of July weekend at Caesar Cardini's Caesar's Palace restaurant in Tijuana, Mexico. The apocryphal tale, often told of spur-of-the-moment culinary inventions, is that on this particular busy weekend, Cardini was running low on food. And so, staring into his icebox, he tossed together a salad for his guests from what was left over. Whatever the truth of the matter may be, the salad quickly traveled north of the border, and turned into a hallmark of tony dining establishments, where it was usually made at tableside with many a flourish and grand gesture. Bottles of Cardini's Original Caesar Dressing can be found to this day in better markets.

---

* **2 heads romaine lettuce**
* **2 eggs**
* **4 tablespoons extra virgin olive oil**
* **salt and coarsely ground pepper**
* **1 tablespoon lemon juice**
* **1 teaspoon Worcestershire sauce**
* **1/4 cup grated Parmesan cheese**
* **2 cups garlic croutons**
* **4 anchovies (optional)**

Tear washed and dried lettuce leaves into long manageable strips. Place in large bowl (aluminum, wood or glass, as you wish). Soft boil eggs for not much longer than one minute; you want them runny. Break the eggs into lettuce (remembering to remove the shells), add oil, salt and pepper, lemon juice (freshly squeezed, if you wish), Worcestershire sauce (which gives the salad its distinctive anchovy flavor) and cheese. Toss joyfully. Add croutons (which you can make yourself, if the mood strikes you, by frying dried bread with garlic, salt and olive oil). (You can also add some anchovy paste, or tinned anchovies, should you be as addicted to fish flavor as I am.)

Serves Four

Clams Casino

In the first decades of the century, if a restaurant wanted to be noted, it came up with a dish that involved the baking of shellfish. Menus of the era are littered with every manner of concoction, most of which involved removing the lobster, crab, oyster or clam from its shell, chopping it with various vegetables, mixing it with an exceedingly rich sauce and returning it to the shell for baking. In a slightly purer form, a vegetable, bread crumb, cream, butter and spirit mixture was spooned over the shellfish and then baked. Clams Casino, a dish born in the restaurant at the Casino at New York's Narragansett Pier, along with oysters Rockefeller, are among the few surviving dishes from the baked shellfish fad. It tastes pleasantly old-fashioned and wonderfully decadent.

---

* **4 tablespoons melted butter**
* **1 tablespoon minced garlic**
* **1 minced shallot**
* **2 tablespoons minced onion**
* **2 tablespoons minced parsley**
* **1/2 teaspoon Tabasco sauce**
* **1/2 teaspoon Worcestershire sauce**
* **2 tablespoons bread crumbs**
* **1 dozen clams on the half shell**
* **3 strips raw bacon**
* **rock salt as needed**

Combine all of the ingredients except the clams, bacon and salt. Mix well, then refrigerate until soft enough to spread atop the open clams. Top each clam with a small piece of bacon. Arrange the clams on rock salt on a cookie sheet and broil for about 4 minutes. When the bacon is done, the dish is ready.

Serves Two

Cobb Salad

The tale of the Cobb is much like that of the Caesar, with an enterprising restaurateur gazing forlornly into his diminished larder and cleverly tossing together what would become a legendary dish through an assiduous use of leftovers. Which is what Bob Cobb's salad certainly sounds like. It's also a salad that, in my humble opinion, has been much improved on over the years. The original Cobb, created in 1926, wasn't so much diced as it was pulverized. This version is chopped much less, so offers far more in terms of bite.

* **1/2 head iceberg lettuce**
* **1/2 head romaine lettuce**
* **1 bunch watercress**
* **a smattering of chicory (or not, if you can't find any)**
* **2 tomatoes**
* **2 broiled chicken breasts**
* **a rasher or two of bacon**
* **1 nice ripe avocado**
* **3 hard-cooked eggs**
* **some chives**
* **1 cup crumbled Roquefort cheese**
* **French dressing**

Chop the lettuces, the watercress (which isn't missed if you don't use it), the chicory (ditto), the tomatoes, chicken, bacon, avocado and eggs into anything from small cubes to a rather tiny dice. Arrange on plate so that it all looks nice and symmetrical. Then toss wildly, adding whatever chopped chives you wish, along with plenty of cheese. French dressing is traditionally a three-to-one mix of oil to vinegar, nicely tarted up with some dried mustard and ground pepper. The original dressing specified red wine vinegar, plus the bite of lemon juice, salt and pepper, Worcestershire, English mustard, and garlic, all to taste.

Serves Four

Crab Louis

No, this classic salad from the twenties wasn't invented by Louis Diat of New
York's Ritz-Carlton. Indeed, it's not even from the East Coast. This is a West
Coast creation, variously claimed by restaurants in San Francisco and Seattle,
whose innovation isn't so much the crab (or shrimp, lobster or artichoke) that this
dish is often built around as it is the mayonnaise and cream sauce that totally
dominates the structure. (Sauce Louis could be spread on old shoes, and they'd
probably taste pretty good.) As with most of the salads that rose to high
popularity in the Roaring Twenties, this one makes the idea of a low-fat diet
seem downright un-American. Bolsheviks were thin; Americans were round
and prosperous, as God intended them to be.

* **1 cup mayonnaise**
* **2 tablespoons heavy cream**
* **1/2 cup chili sauce**
* **1 tablespoon Tabasco sauce**
* **1 teaspoon Worcestershire**
* **1 teaspoon horseradish**
* **2 tablespoons chopped olives**
* **2 tablespoons chopped scallions**
* **2 tablespoons lemon juice**
* **salt and pepper**
* **shredded lettuce**
* **crabmeat/lobster meat/bay**
  shrimp/artichoke bottoms
* **sliced hard-cooked eggs**

Combine all of the ingredients from
the mayonnaise to the salt and pepper.
Mix until smooth. Taste and adjust the
seasonings. Arrange the crabmeat,
lobster, shrimp or artichoke bottoms
atop a bed of lettuce. Garnish with
sliced eggs. Sauce liberally.

Serves Four

Green Goddess Dressing

As further proof that the twenties were the Age of the Salad, the chefs of the decade also gave us the remarkably intense and, unfortunately, nearly forgotten Green Goddess Dressing. This dressing is widely reported as a creation of the Palace Hotel in San Francisco, either in honor of, or at the suggestion of, crusty actor George Arliss, who was starring in a play called The Green Goddess. *A dressing that combines anchovies and tarragon vinegar is a bit strong for modern tastes. This seems to be one of those dishes that worked best in an age when people smoked; the powerful flavors did much to cut through tobacco-deadened tastebuds.*

---

* **2 cups mayonnaise**
* **1 small can anchovy filets**
* **3 finely chopped scallions**
* **1 tablespoon minced garlic**
* **2 tablespoons chopped parsley**
* **1 tablespoon lemon juice**
* **1/4 cup tarragon vinegar**
* **salt and pepper**
* **1/2 cup sour cream or yogurt**

Combine all ingredients until smooth and pleasant. Spoon over romaine lettuce and top with shredded chicken, bay shrimp or lump crabmeat.

Serves Four

Icebox Cheese Pie

With the introduction of home refrigerators — or at least inexpensive and readily available ice — dishes that could be "cooked" in the chill achieved popularity. There are a multitude of icebox pies (and icebox cookies as well), one of the most popular of which was a sort of cheesecake in a pie crust made overnight in the fridge.

* **2 tablespoons Knox unflavored gelatin**
* **1 cup cold water**
* **4 eggs**
* **3/4 cup sugar**
* **3 cups whipped cream cheese**
* **3 tablespoons chocolate sauce**
* **1 cup heavy cream**
* **1 9-inch pie crust (graham-cracker crust works fine)**

Dissolve the gelatin in the cold water. Separate the egg yolks and whites. Combine the egg yolks and half the sugar and heat briefly, stirring constantly. Add gelatin and water to the yolks and sugar, stirring well until the gelatin is fully dissolved. Remove from heat. Beat together the cream cheese and chocolate. Add the egg mixture and continue beating until smooth. Beat the egg whites with the remaining sugar until stiff peaks form. Combine with the yolk and cheese mixture. Whip the cream and fold it in. Pour into the crust and refrigerate until firm, usually overnight.

Serves Eight

Bavarian Jell-O Dessert with Fruit

I've long argued that Jell-O is the single greatest culinary creation of the twentieth century. And as we come to the final years, I see no reason to change my mind. The roots of Jell-O go back to 1845, when it was patented by one Peter Cooper, who described it as a "transparent concentrated substance containing all the ingredients fitting it for table use in a potable form, and requiring only the addition of hot water to dissolve it so that it may be poured into moulds, and when it is cold will be fit for use." Which sounds exactly like what we're eating a century and a half later. The product was dubbed Jell-O in 1897 by Mary Wait, wife of cough medicine manufacturer Pearl Wait, who sold the name for four-hundred-fifty dollars in 1899 to a neighbor. By the 1920s, sales reached the millions, Jell-O salads were ubiquitous, and Jell-O had become the most American of foods. The symbolic implications are best left untouched. Recipes abound, from the basic method found on the side of the box to varia-tions using Coca-Cola, cream cheese, mixed nuts, Red Hots, marshmallows, tomato juice and vinegar, applesauce and even a Jell-O dessert made with Twinkies, reported on by Jane and Michael Stern in their book Square Meals. *Jell-O may be the last true frontier for the adventurous cook.*

---

* **1 4-serving package of Jell-O, any flavor**
* **1 cup boiling water**
* **1 cup ice-cold water**
* **2 cups whipped cream**
* **1 cup fresh fruit (anything except pineapple, kiwi, mango, papaya or figs)**

In the time-honored fashion, dissolve gelatin in boiling water. Add the cold water, then the fruit. Fold in 1-1/2 cups whipped cream (feel free to substitute Cool Whip). Spoon into cups or a 4-cup mold. Chill until firm. Top with remaining cream.

Serves Four

Lemon Chess Pie

Though the roots of lemon chess pie stretch deep into the nineteenth century, it wasn't until the 1920s that it became a standard at the diners and roadside restaurants of America. There is a good reason for its popularity: it's a remarkably easy pie to make, one that even the most inept cook can turn out without too much difficulty.

* **2 cups sugar**
* **1 tablespoon cornmeal**
* **1 tablespoon all-purpose flour**
* **1/4 cup melted butter**
* **1/4 cup light cream**
* **4 eggs**
* **juice of 2 lemons**
* **grated lemon rind**
* **pinch of salt**
* **1 9-inch pie shell**

Combine all of the ingredients, except, of course, the pie shell. Mix until smooth and moist. Spoon into the unbaked pie shell (the frozen ones work very well, and graham cracker crusts are good too). Bake at 350 degrees for 40 minutes. Serve with vanilla ice cream.

Serves Four

The Martini

The definitive cocktail of the twenties is claimed by any of a dozen sources, most of which made a drink that bears little resemblance to the mixture of gin and vermouth, served with or without an olive, that became the hallmark of sophisticated drinking in the year before Prohibition. Whether it was invented in San Francisco's Occidental Hotel or in the San Francisco Bay Area town of Martinez or came into being through the Italian vermouth importer later known as Martini & Rossi (among many possible derivations), the original Martini was anything but dry. Early recipes tended to combine gin with a large quantity of sweet vermouth and, often, maraschino liqueur — a drink closer to a Mai Tai than a modern-day Martini. But by the twenties, it had evolved into the drink that no sophisticate was ever far from, with a range of gadgets and devices for making the perfect Martini that persist to this day. I suspect that the most important parts of the process are the right glass and nice plump olives. My favorite recipe, simple as pie, perfect as the universe, follows:

---

* **2 ounces of the best dry gin (Bombay Sapphire is excellent)**
* **1/2 ounce very dry vermouth**
* **2 olives**

Ice the shaker. Add the gin and vermouth. Stir (do not shake, for it bruises the gin). Ice the glass. Strain in the liquor. Gently add olives.

Serves One

Reuben Sandwich

The credit for this dish goes to Arnold Reuben of the legendary Reuben's Deli in New York City, a landmark that was the Carnegie Deli before there was a Carnegie Deli. Those of us who ate there before the place closed in the sixties remember it as the home of the definitive Reuben sandwich — big, greasy, overwhelming and absolutely delicious.

* **2 thick slices of rye bread**
* **mustard**
* **1/4 pound sliced corned beef**
* **1/4 pound sliced Swiss cheese**
* **sauerkraut**
* **2 tablespoons butter**

Spread the mustard on the bread, top and bottom. Layer the Swiss cheese on the bottom, then the corned beef, then Swiss cheese, then a layer of sauerkraut, then more Swiss cheese. In a hot pan, melt the butter and fry the sandwich first on one side, then flip it and fry on the other, until the cheese melts and holds the sandwich together.

Serves One

Crash Courses
1930~1940

On October 29, 1929, the Dow-Jones Industrial Average plunged 30.57 points, a seemingly insignificant amount today but enough back then to send the stock market into a panic, based not so much on the actual drop in value as on the massive degree to which speculators had bought their stocks on margin. It was time to pay up. And since the money earned had all been spent during the happy days of the twenties, it wasn't there. An estimated $30 billion was called for. When it didn't materialize, the whole financial house of cards that had been the previous decade collapsed. All too real was the now-clichéd image of the distraught businessmen who threw themselves from office windows. The great status symbol of the thirties was having a job. Three hots and a cot became a national dream.

It was a decade when culinary expectations were very definitely diminished. Nonetheless, they also definitely existed. The films of the time, cranked out by the perpetually optimistic Hollywood dream machine, were fond of showing people, dressed in tuxedos and long gowns, elegantly sipping their Manhattans, Old-Fashioneds, Rob Roys and, of course, Martinis. One of my favorite cinematic moments, repeated over and over again, was in the various *Thin Man* movies. William Powell and Myrna Loy, each dressed in layers of pajamas and robes, lying in their single beds with a night table between them, would sip a nightcap dispensed from a silver shaker into perfectly chilled glasses. There was no evidence that they ever had sex. But they sure did drink.

Prohibition was finally repealed in 1933, which may or may not have been related to the start of the Great Depression. In its own way, America seems to have been preparing itself in the late 1920s for a decade of privation. Velveeta cheese (a definitively down-scale, po' folks food) was introduced in 1928, at about the same time that sliced bread became the national standard. Popeye appeared in his first comic strip in 1929, positioning inexpensive canned spinach as something that was good to eat (it is, though nothing tastes quite as canned as canned spinach).

In 1929 the po' boy sandwich earned its name during a streetcar strike in New Orleans. Hostess Twinkies, the perfect trailer park snack, was born in 1930. White Castle Burgers — endearing, addictive slivers of meat and filler topped with a pickle slice, fried onions and ketchup and served on a soft bun — began to spread across the eastern United States, selling for a nickel each. ("Buy 'em by the bagful!") It's not without significance that in 1930, fabled French chef Auguste Escoffier prepared a grand gala of a meal at the new Hotel Pierre, while the very downscale Chock Full o' Nuts coffee-and-sandwich shops opened their first branches.

Italian-American restaurants spread from coast to coast in the thirties, providing good, inexpensive food in an era when money was in short supply. Since meals that stretched the dollar were in demand, the single defining dish of the age may well have been macaroni and cheese casserole. It was cheap, easy to make and very filling. It was, in essence, a reasonable substitute for meat, which few Americans could afford.

Though the word casserole comes from the French *casse*, meaning "ladle," which in turn comes from the Greek word *kyath* meaning a "cup," the concept of casserole cooking was raised to its zenith during the Great Depression, not so much because casserole cooking is a wondrous way of preparing food but because this pseudo-elegant stew allowed a hungry nation to make something out of little. The trick was to put lots of things into the pot, stretching the expensive protein with cheaper vegetables and grains. Instead of a stew, a casserole was cooking in the oven, allowing flavors to communicate with and improve each other, turning left-overs into a gourmet meal. With the judicious addition of enough seasoning and a crispy top, any casserole tastes good.

It was also a decade when many substitutes were accepted as almost as good as the real thing. There was mock apple pie, in which inexpensive Ritz crackers were substituted for more expensive apples. American chop suey, popular in

the twenties and thirties, was made with hamburger, tomato and elbow macaroni. There was the Shirley Temple, a nonalcoholic drink that did its very best to look alcoholic. It was an age filled with ersatz foreign-sounding foods that had little meaning in their supposed lands of origin — English muffins, Swiss cheese, French fries, Spanish rice, Danish pastry, Russian tea, Turkish taffy, French toast, Welsh rabbit, Canadian bacon, Russian dressing, Bavarian cream, brussels sprouts, Scotch woodcock, Bombay duck and Dutch goose. There was a sense that things were being sort of gussied up in a national effort to make more out of less. To stretch. To make ends meet.

Despite the Big Depression — or perhaps because of it — American innovation ran along at high speed. In 1930, Birdseye Brand Frosted Foods (as they were rather reticently called) went on sale for the first time. Few Americans had anything more advanced than an icebox, and the iceman, delivering blocks of ice that melted into pans beneath the ice boxes, remained a familiar figure. Still, by the middle of the decade, home freezers were becoming commercially important and frozen food sales were on the increase. Suddenly, thanks to a determined Clarence Birdseye, almost every manner of vegetable and every manner of cuisine, for that matter, was available to anyone with a freezer. This seemingly simple fact profoundly changed the way Americans would eat for the rest of the century.

It was also the decade that prepackaged, presliced Wonder Bread hit the stores, changing forever the Americans' relationship with their daily bread. Bisquick was introduced, allowing home bakers to make biscuits that seemed to never, ever fail. Fritos corn chips were born, along with Skippy Peanut Butter, Pepperidge Farm Bread, Spam, prune juice and Ritz crackers. So were Snickers bars, 3 Musketeers bars and Lay's potato chips. The world tasted its first Campbell's Chicken Noodle Soup and Cream of Mushroom Soup — and who could imagine the world without either? Following hard on the heels of the end of Prohibition in 1933, the first branch of Alcoholics Anonymous was formed in 1935.

In August 1930, Michael Cullen opened the King Kullen market in Jamaica, Long Island. In 1936, the Waring Blender was introduced by bandleader Fred Waring (as in Fred Waring's Pennsylvanians — remember "Little White Lies" and "I Found a Million Dollar Baby in a Five-and-Ten-Cent Store"?). After centuries of grinding, pounding, mashing and stirring things by hand, you could drop just about anything into the blender and have it liquified in an instant. It didn't simply make mixing exotic drinks easier (though that certainly was a pleasant benefit), it opened up a wide world of chopped foods for the modern chef of the 1930s. Indeed, along with the toaster, the blender was one of the first significant electric kitchen appliances — a big step on the road to the all-electric kitchen of the fifties.

The year 1936 was also the year of *Joy of Cooking*, perhaps the single most successful cookbook in American history. Originally written by a St. Louis housewife named Irma S. Rombauer (and later revised and updated by her daughter, Marion Rombauer Becker), *Joy of Cooking* is equaled only by *The James Beard Cookbook* when it comes to absolutely nailing down recipes for the ambitious yet not widely experienced household cook. Ingredients are listed with medical exactitude, cooking instructions given with military precision. And there's hardly a recipe you might want to create that isn't in *Joy*. It emerged from the Depression out of a need to improve the way we eat through, as one chapter points out, "knowledge." Two-thirds of a century later, it's still the definitive way to learn to cook

In the middle of 1937, researchers at the Ford Motor Company came up with a vegetable protein that could be turned into a product that tasted enough like animal protein to create a major new industry of soy products, among them the first artificial bacon. In that same year, the first supermarket shopping cart was crafted by market owner Sylvan Goldman in Oklahoma City, Oklahoma. It allowed shoppers to pick up far more groceries in a single visit than they could ever manage before, adding a great sense of abundance to the growing American mania for home cooking. And in 1938 Teflon was developed by a DuPont chemist — a product that would seriously affect the cooking of the sixties and seventies, as Americans discovered that fat-free cuisine was a distinct possibility. In 1939, National Presto Industries unveiled the pressure cooker at the New York World's Fair and proclaimed it as the next big thing in home cooking.

By the end of the thirties, the effects of the Depression were diminishing with lockstep regularity. Americans were spending more, buying more, eating better. The Waldorf-Astoria Hotel had opened in New York in 1931, setting a new standard for cuisine at a time when few could afford it. By the end of the decade, that standard had spread throughout the major cities. In the years that followed, Cafe des Artistes, the Rainbow Room and Gallagher's Steak House opened in New York; Perino's, Chasen's, Lawry's Prime Rib and Don the Beachcomber opened in Los Angeles; Ernie's and Trader Vic's opened in San Francisco. The stage was set for an age of fine dining. Unfortunately, the stage was also set for the most horrifying war in world history. ★

The Perfect Margarita (as prepared at Trader Vic's)

Of this we can be sure: no one knows for certain where the first Margarita was mixed, poured and imbibed. One popular tale says it's the creation of a bartender named Daniel Negrete of the Garcia Crespo Hotel in Puebla, Mexico, who named it for his girlfriend, a woman with a penchant for taking a lick of salt before downing her tequila. Other stories credit the drink to Margarita Sames, a rich rancher in San Antonio, Texas, who always served it to her guests. Some say it was invented by Dona Bertha of Bertita's Bar in Taxco, Mexico, around 1930. And there's a plaque in the clubhouse of the Agua Caliente Racetrack in Tijuana claiming the Margarita was invented there. What we do know for sure is that they drank a lot of them in the thirties. And we drink a lot of them today. To make a great one takes nothing but some very good ingredients and a lot of ice.

* **juice of half a lime**
* **half an ounce of Triple Sec**
* **one ounce of tequila**
* **salt**

Shake with ice cubes. Strain into chilled champagne glass with salt around the rim. Drink. Look out.

Serves One

Cherries Jubilee

Although it was introduced by August Escoffier, chef at London's Carleton House, to celebrate Queen Victoria's Diamond Jubilee, this fabled dessert had its biggest blaze of glory in dining rooms across America several decades later. Beginning in the thirties, mostly in restaurants at first and then increasingly in homes, cherries jubilee was accepted as the ultimate festive dessert, proof that the maker was a master of the culinary arts. It singlehandedly created a market for kirsch in America. It tastes good to this day, though flaming dishes in modern homes have an unfortunate tendency to set off the smoke alarms.

* **1 can pitted cherries in syrup (black cherries are usually called for, but any type will do)**
* **1-1/2 tablespoons cornstarch**
* **2 tablespoons sugar**
* **1/2 cup kirsch (though brandy will suffice)**
* **1 pint vanilla ice cream**

Drain the cherries, reserving the syrup. Mix the cornstarch with the syrup until dissolved, then stir in the sugar. Heat over a low flame, stirring constantly. Pour the sauce over the cherries. Warm kirsch in a saucepan, then pour over the cherries. With great care, ignite the kirsch. Ladle the flaming cherries over the ice cream. Serve, remembering to let the flame burn out before eating.

Serves Four

Chicken Cacciatore

Like cioppino, chop suey and vichyssoise, this notably tasty dish of chicken significantly spiced up with lots of good sauce is little known in the land from which it would seem to have sprung. True, cacciatora (hunter's style) is an acceptable Italian cooking style, but the Italian-American preparation of chicken cacciatore (with mushrooms and tomato sauce) isn't the chicken cacciatora found in Italy. Along with lasagna, ravioli and spaghetti with meatballs, it's one of the keystones of Italian-American restaurant cooking. Although many Italian cooks made their own sauce, many busy mamas in the thirties used the likes of Contadina, which bottled its first sauce in 1918.

---

* ★ 2 quartered chickens
* ★ olive oil as needed
* ★ 2 chopped onions
* ★ 2 tablespoons of minced garlic
* ★ 1 large bottle spaghetti sauce of your choice
* ★ 1 glass red wine (you choose the size of that glass)
* ★ 1 tablespoon oregano
* ★ 3 bay leaves
* ★ 1 chopped green pepper
* ★ 1 pound sliced mushrooms
* ★ salt and pepper

Brown the chicken pieces in olive oil. Mix the remaining ingredients in a pan, cooking for about half an hour, or until they smell really good. Pour half of the sauce into a roasting pan. Add the chicken. Top with the remainder of sauce. Bake at 375 degrees for 60 minutes. Serve over spaghetti.

Serves Four to Six

Cioppino

It's said that this massive seafood stew was created in the thirties on the docks of San Francisco. At the end of the day, go the tales, the Italian fishermen would gather on the pier to talk about their luck at sea and to prepare a big pot of stew over a fire started as a bulwark against the evening's chill. If you wanted to eat from the stew pot, you had to "chip in" some seafood. In time, the term took on a comic Italian sound — "chip-in-o," which evolved into the name as we know it, cioppino. The story may be apocryphal, for there's a Genoese fish stew called cioppin. But that's not nearly as romantic as chip-in-o. The dish began to appear on restaurant menus in San Francisco. Eventually, it spread so far and wide that it comes as a great surprise to diners to discover it was born in San Francisco rather than Naples. Like most stews, it's a dish that's hard to ruin — the more you chip in, the better it becomes.

---

* 1/4 cup olive oil
* 6 quartered onions
* 12 mashed garlic cloves
* 1 large can peeled tomatoes
* 1 small can tomato puree
* 4 stalks celery, sliced
* 1 tablespoon dried oregano
* 4 bay leaves
* 1/2 tablespoon dried thyme
* 1/2 tablespoon dried sage
* 1 tablespoon fresh parsley
* 4 cups stock (fish stock is best, but chicken stock will do)
* shrimp
* crabmeat
* clams
* mussels
* scallops
* oysters
* fish filets
* 2 glasses red wine
* salt and pepper
* Italian bread

In a large pot, slowly saute the onions and garlic in the olive oil. Add the tomatoes, tomato puree, celery, herbs and stock. When it's all nice and hot, add the shellfish and wine. Bring to a boil and simmer for half an hour or more, adding the fish filets late in the cooking process to avoid cooking so long that the fish falls to pieces. Serve over thick slices of toasted Italian bread.

Serves Eight to Twelve

Dagwood Sandwich

In the early thirties, a young comic-strip character named Dagwood Bumstead married a flapper who went by the moniker of Blondie Boobadoop. The result of that union was two children — Alexander and Cookie — along with a dog named Daisy and America's greatest sandwich. The only thing Dagwood prepared in the kitchen, was, according to his creator, Chic Young, a mountainous pile of dissimilar leftovers precariously arranged between two slices of bread. Some have gone so far as to label it as compensatory male behavior, like the skyscraper, an act of aggression. Regular guy that I am, I tend to see the Dagwood in simpler terms. Sometimes a big sandwich is just a big sandwich. I love the way its construct is absolutely freeform — whatever is sitting in the fridge is fair game. Hold the anchovies, though.

---

* **sliced rye bread**
* **luncheon meats**
* **sliced cheeses**
* **mustard**
* **mayonnaise**
* **relish**
* **pickles**

Layer the meats and cheeses atop one slice of bread until there's far too much to eat. Spread mustard and mayonnaise on the second slice of bread. Top the meat and cheese with relish. Place the second slice of bread atop the sandwich. Attach a pickle with a toothpick. Eat with care.

Serves One or more

Macaroni 'n' Cheese

In 1937, the Kraft Food Company, which had introduced processed cheese to the world in 1915, released its macaroni and cheese package, known to the world as "Kraft Dinner." As America slowly emerged from the Depression, it became the housewife's friend — a nourishing one-pot meal that could be easily prepared and that kids loved. In the years since, Kraft Dinner has taken on a life of its own, a meal of macaroni and cheese that doesn't quite taste like anything else in the world. And with sales of 300 million boxes a year, it doesn't have to. For the record, though, it is possible to actually make macaroni and cheese from scratch. It has lots of texture and nice stretchy cheese. But fans of Kraft Dinner may find it a bit daunting — it's a lot of work to make.

---

* **1 pound elbow macaroni**
* **water as needed**
* **6 tablespoons margarine**
* **1/2 cup all-purpose flour**
* **4 cups milk**
* **3 cups shredded Cheddar cheese**
* **salt and pepper**

Cook the macaroni until it's tender. Drain it and put aside.

Melt four tablespoons of margarine. Blend in the flour, stir in milk, and add two cups of shredded cheese. Simmer until the cheese melts, adding salt and pepper to taste.

Mix the macaroni with the cheese sauce. Pour into a greased casserole. Mash together the remaining margarine and cheese and sprinkle the mixture over the macaroni. Bake at 350 degrees for 30 minutes. Serve when brown and bubbly.

Serves Eight

Mock Apple Pie

Thanks to the promotional efforts of the folks who made Ritz crackers, this dish using the crackers as an inexpensive alternative to apples was one of the definitive dishes of the thirties. For years, the recipe has appeared on the back of the Ritz Cracker box, even though apples have cost less than Ritz Crackers for quite some time now. What's really amazing about this recipe is just how good it tastes — and how much the texture resembles that of apples. It's one of those dishes that all home cooks should make at least once in their lifetime, just to say they've actually done it.

---

* **sufficient pastry for a two-crust 9-inch pie**
* **36 Ritz Crackers, broken into small bits**
* **1 cup water**
* **2 cups sugar**
* **2 teaspoons cream of tartar**
* **2 tablespoons lemon juice**
* **grated rind of one lemon**
* **2 tablespoons margarine**
* **1/2 teaspoon cinnamon**
* **1/4 teaspoon nutmeg**
* **no apples**

Line a 9-inch pastry dish with half of the crust. Sprinkle in the cracker bits. Bring the water, cream of tartar and sugar to a boil and simmer for 15 minutes. Add the lemon juice and rind to the resulting syrup and pour over the crackers. Dot with margarine, sprinkle with cinnamon and nutmeg. Top with the remaining pastry; trim, seal and flute the edges. Slit the top. Bake at 425 degrees for 30 minutes, or until the crust is crisp and golden. Cool and serve.

Serves Six

Oxtail Soup

One of the culinary benefits of the Depression was an increased interest in using parts that were formerly looked down upon as rather low-rent. Tripe went through a brief spurt of popularity, as did kidneys, heart, liver and oxtail, which found its way onto many a menu as oxtail soup, a dish that could be presented with elegance in a fine downtown restaurant or as a daily special in a country roadhouse. As it turns out, properly flavored, it's a delicious concoction if a bit on the gamy side.

* **2 pounds disjointed oxtail**
* **1/4 cup olive oil**
* **8 cups chicken stock**
* **4 diced potatoes**
* **2 chopped onions**
* **4 chopped celery stalks**
* **6 tablespoons butter**
* **3 tablespoons all-purpose flour**
* **2 tablespoons chopped parsley**
* **2 teaspoons dried marjoram**
* **1/2 teaspoon dried thyme**
* **1/4 teaspoon cayenne pepper**
* **salt and pepper**

Heat olive oil. Braise oxtail joints in oil until brown — be bold and the flavor will increase. Add chicken stock and cook the oxtail joints for one hour. In a separate pot, saute the potatoes, onions and celery in melted butter until they're tender. Add the flour and blend till smooth. Combine the oxtails and broth with the vegetables. Bring to a boil, add the herbs and spices. Simmer for about half an hour. Serve hot with thick-crusted bread.

Serves Eight

Tamale Pie

For anyone traveling through the southwest in the thirties, this ubiquitous concoction wasn't just an occasional meal; it was often dinner night after night in small roadhouses where tamale pie was often the single most palatable dish on the menu. It's a gut bomb of cornmeal mush, filled with chopped meat and chili sauce — the hotter the better. Somehow the cornmeal seems to keep the chili under control. Otherwise, it would be pure poison, as fine a cause of indigestion as you'll ever find on a plate.

---

* 1 cup yellow cornmeal
* pinch cayenne pepper
* pinch salt
* 6 cups water
* 1 chopped onion
* 2 tablespoons Gebhardt's chili powder
* 2 tablespoons oil (lard if you can bear it)
* 2 cups chopped meat
* 2 cups canned tomatoes
* 1 chopped green pepper
* 1 tablespoon crushed garlic
* bottled hot sauce

Combine the cornmeal, pepper, salt, and water, bring to a boil, and cook 45 minutes or until the cornmeal mush is so thick that it pulls away from the sides of the pot. Fry the onions with the chili powder in oil. Add the meat, and fry thoroughly. Add the tomatoes, and sprinkle in all the hot sauce you can possibly tolerate. Line an oiled casserole dish with the cornmeal mush, scoop the meat mixture into the center, and bake in a 350 degree oven for one hour. Serve with more hot sauce.

Serves Six

Toll House Cookies

It's rare that the origin of a dish can be pinpointed with absolute accuracy. Such is the case, however, of the Toll House cookie, invented by Mrs. Ruth Whitfield in the kitchen of the Toll House Inn of Whitman, Massachusetts, soon after she and her husband purchased the eighteenth-century landmark in 1930. Making a cookie she'd often baked before, called a Butter Drop-Do, she added some chunks of Nestlé Semi-Sweet Chocolate that were on hand. The cookies became a sensation at her inn and spread so quickly that by 1939, the Nestlé Company had introduced a line of Semi-Sweet Chocolate Morsels (read: chocolate chips) to keep up with the demand. The company also printed the recipe for Toll House Cookies on the bag, where you'll find it to this very day.

---

* **2-1/4 cups unsifted flour**
* **1 teaspoon baking soda**
* **1 teaspoon salt**
* **1 cup butter**
* **3/4 cup granulated sugar**
* **3/4 cup brown sugar**
* **1 teaspoon vanilla**
* **2 whole eggs**
* **12 ounces Nestlé Semi-Sweet Chocolate Morsels**
* **1 cup chopped nuts**

In one bowl, combine the flour, baking soda and salt. In another bowl, mix together the butter, sugars and vanilla. Beat well, then add the eggs. Combine with the flour mixture until smooth. Stir in chocolate chips and chopped nuts. Drop spoonfuls onto an ungreased cookie sheet. Bake at 375 degrees for ten minutes.

Makes about 100 cookies

Victory and M&Ms
1940~1950

I t is notable that four of the ten decades of the twentieth century are defined, more than anything else, by their wars. There was the Great War of the 1910s. The Korean conflict of the 1950s. The Vietnam imbroglio of the 1960s. And, more than any other, World War II of the 1940s. With still imperfect twenty-twenty hindsight, World War II seems to have had a more significant influence on our culinary habits than any other period of strife, including the American Revolution and the Civil War, both fought on our native soil.

Sales of convenience foods increased as domestic servants and housewives went to work in war plants. The first half of the decade was also, thanks to the war, a time of food rationing and hoarding of sugar, coffee, butter and cheese. Meat was rationed, too, limited at the beginning of the war to 28 ounces a week per person. But production rose by 50 percent and so did consumption, to 128.9 pounds per capita annually as the wartime economy put more money in workers' pockets. The consumption of fresh vegetables dropped as frozen food became readily available in grocery stores.

Overall, it was a time of making do. People stretched foodstuffs as much as they could, making a little go a long way. In *How to Cook a Wolf*, M.F.K. Fisher helped Americans cope with wartime food and servant shortages and condoned the use of frozen and canned vegetables. Cooking a steak in batter made it a lot more filling than a steak cooked by itself. Mixing Fritos corn chips with chili resulted in a dish of stretcher (chili) that was in itself stretched. The Philadelphia cheesesteak was a brilliant way of making a very small amount of not very good quality beef seem like a lot of food. And the corn dog, one of the great creations of the age, was a remarkable way of making the intrinsically inexpensive hot dog go a very long distance. In 1942, its creators, vaudevillians Neil and Carl Fletcher of Dallas, Texas, managed to find a batter that was both edible and would stay on the frankfurter. They sold their corn dogs at the Texas state fair.

And then there was Spam. The world's best-selling canned meat was created, according to the official company line, in 1937, by Jay C. Hormel, son of George A. Hormel, as a way of using pork shoulder left over from Hormel's other products. According to the label, chopped pork shoulder is mixed with "ham meat, salt, water, sugar and sodium nitrite." The result was a cube of salty meat that could become just about anything. (A recipe on the can suggests scoring it like a ham, glazing it with a jam-and-mustard sauce and baking it. I've done it — it was disturbingly tasty.) Because it's cooked in the can, it has a seven-year shelf life, at least.

During World War II, it became a battle-front favorite. Soviet premier Nikita Khrushchev later praised it as the food "without which we could not have been able to feed our army." Inevitably, its use spilled over into civilian cookery.

It was in the 1940s that Cheerios were born, along with Maxwell House Instant Coffee, Kellogg's Raisin Bran, Almond Joy, Reddi-Whip, V-8, Sara Lee Cheesecake and the Baskin-Robbins ice cream chain. And perhaps as a symbol of the end of rationing — a time during which even the production of sliced bread was banned in order to prevent waste — in 1945, C.A. Swanson & Sons began a line of canned and frozen chicken and turkey products that would lead to the introduction of the TV dinner in 1954.

Former DuPont chemist Earl W. Tupper started selling a line of plastic containers that didn't leak and kept food fresh for a surprisingly long time. He called it Tupperware. And in a marketing coup of awesome proportions, it would be sold at Tupperware home parties, one of the defining events of the decade to come.

But the two main icons of the decade stand alone. In 1940, as clouds gathered over Europe and the Pacific, Richard and Maurice McDonald opened their first hamburger stand in a drive-in movie theater in San Bernardino, California, east of Los Angeles. The other grew out of the military's desire for a candy that didn't melt in warm climates. In 1941, M&Ms were created by Forrest E. Mars and Bruce E. Murrie. What M&Ms and McDonald's say about how — and what — we ate back then is encyclopedic. They are world-class culinary symbols of their age. Indeed, they probably made Jung very happy.

In purely symbolic terms, the M&M was the very essence of America in 1941. It had a hard shell, the valiant defender of the chocolate within. It was designed to stand up to both heat ("The milk chocolate that melts in your mouth, not in your hands") and to cold (frozen M&Ms taste quite as good as those at room temperature; they just crunch a lot more). It's the American answer to the Rock of Gibraltar. It's the Maginot Line that doesn't crumble. It's the shield on the *Enterprise*, unbreakable by the vilest of Klingon measures. For those fighting in World War II, it was solid proof that America would persevere: If we could make a candy shell impervious to any foe, stopping Hitler and Hirohito would be easy. Like a battleship or a fighter plane, it was clearly marked as what it was — there was a tiny "M" printed on the shell of every single candy, always perfectly placed, applied with a vegetable ink by a process the company will only say is "akin to offset printing." It came in a variety of colors, none of which were offensive to the eye — brown, orange, tan, yellow, red, green, more recently blue (along with a variety of new holiday colors for Easter and Christmas). It could have been the colors of a national flag.

And within, protected by the hard shell, was a solid chunk of all-American chocolate, God Bless America chocolate, and maybe a peanut. The M&M is all that made America great in one tidy little package. Only Jell-O is a greater creation. And Jell-O with M&M pieces dropped within is a bit of nationalism filled with amazing possibilities. True believers could march against the very armies of Hell properly fueled with Jell-O and M&Ms.

McDonald's is, of course, a symbol of far greater complexity. In 1940, it was nothing more than a place to get a burger in a drive-in. By 1948 it had turned into a self-service restaurant where the burgers were cranked out fast and cheap and served hot — and where the already cooked French fries were kept warm by newly installed infrared lamps. It was the right restaurant at the right time. Coming on the heels of World War II, it satisfied our growing national need for food on the road, along with a growing obsession with getting things done fast. (Very possibly, after losing half a decade to the war, Americans were anxious to catch up.) It was also the right restaurant for a nation that was swiftly shifting from an urban society to a suburban society. For those who spent their days and nights driving along the burgeoning landscape of freeways, heading for the Levittowns of the world, the sight of the Golden Arches was a friendly beacon, a light in the wilderness that assured good burgers, fries and malts. It also, in its own symbolic fashion, as both a signifier and a thing signified, lit the way into the next decade for a generation born in a time between wars. It was to be a decade of conspicuous consumption unlike any other the world has known. And a decade that was merely the first of many when we ate not to live, but lived mostly to eat. ★

Pumpkin Chiffon Pie

There's no clear agreement about just how chiffon pie became one of the

definitive desserts of the post-World War II years. The only thing that's really

clear is that everyone, but everyone, was making them. Women's magazines of

the time were thick with chiffon recipes — not just chiffon pies, but chiffon

cakes, chiffon puddings, all of which cleverly combined gelatin with egg whites

and egg yolks into a frothy, light, sweet concoction that just about anyone could

make, and just about everyone did. The variations seem infinite. But the most

popular in the forties was the pumpkin chiffon pie, which has oddly faded from

favor. One taste, and you'll wonder, as we did, why we ever lost our taste for

such a terrific heap of sweetness.

---

* **1 pre-baked pie shell**
* **1 tablespoon unflavored gelatin**
* **1/4 cup cold water**
* **4 egg yolks**
* **3/4 cup sugar**
* **1-1/2 cups canned pumpkin**
* **1/4 cup light cream**
* **1/4 teaspoon cinnamon**
* **1/4 teaspoon allspice**
* **4 egg whites**
* **whipped cream**

Dissolve the gelatin in water. Beat the egg yolks, then add the sugar, pumpkin, cream and spices. Cook in a double boiler till thickened. Stir in the dissolved gelatin. Whip the egg whites until they form stiff peaks. Fold the egg whites into pumpkin mixture. Fill the pie crust and chill. Top with whipped cream just before serving.

Serves Six

Marinara Sauce

While millions of American servicemen came back from the war in the Pacific, millions more returned from Europe with a taste for the foods they had experienced over there. For the most part French cooking, which intimidated American taste buds, was left behind. But Italian cuisine, which Americans had encountered earlier in the form of Italian-American cuisine, traveled well. Those who served in Italy developed a taste for stronger sauces, more herbs, more spices. Marinara sauce became the flavor of choice in the late forties for just about every dish of spaghetti (which was on its way to becoming "pasta") cooking in America.

---

* ★ 1/4 cup olive oil
* ★ 1 chopped onion
* ★ 2 tablespoons minced garlic
* ★ 1/2 pound sliced mushrooms
* ★ 1 glass red wine
* ★ 4 cups peeled, chopped tomatoes
* ★ 1 teaspoon dried basil
* ★ 1 teaspoon dried oregano
* ★ 1 teaspoon sugar
* ★ salt and pepper

Saute the onions, garlic and mushrooms. Add the remainder of the ingredients and cook for an hour, or until the smell drives you half mad with hunger. Ladle over freshly cooked pasta, and top with freshly grated Parmesan.

Serves Six

The Bloody Mary

In a decade when a good strong drink was called for, this classic combination of
vodka, tomato juice and seasonings was a beverage with both muscle and
vitamins. Along with the restorative effects of vodka, you got your vitamin C.
Harry's New York Bar in Paris, the King Cole Bar at the St. Regis in New York,
several spots in Chicago and an assortment of places in San Francisco claim to be
the drink's first home. The Bloody Mary had a major comeback in the seventies
as the perfect accompaniment to Sunday brunch. Unlike the Martini, which works
quite well with either vodka or gin, only vodka will do for a Bloody Mary; the
bastard versions made with gin, rum and tequila are just that. And the more
Tabasco the better; this is supposed to be a drink that grows hair on your chest,
if not on your head.

---

* 1-1/2 ounces vodka
* 1/2 ounce lemon juice
* 3 shakes Tabasco sauce
* 1 shake Worcestershire sauce
* tomato juice to fill
* salt and pepper
* 1 celery stick

Pour the vodka, lemon juice, Tabasco and Worcestershire sauces over ice. Top with the tomato juice. Sprinkle with salt and pepper. Stir with the celery stick. Eat the celery stick if you're hungry. Otherwise, discard it.

Serves One

Chicken-fried Steak

This caloric gutbuster was one of the dishes discovered by soldiers returning from the war in the Pacific, as they journeyed across the Southwest. It's a slab of beef fried like a piece of chicken, which is to say breaded and then cooked a long time. It's served with white gravy. This is not a dish for tender stomachs. It is food for the men (and women) who settled the West.

* **1 6-ounce round steak**
* **1/2 cup all-purpose flour**
* **lard or vegetable oil**
* **salt and pepper**
* **1/4 cup milk**

Pound the steak until it's thin and reasonably tender. Sprinkle with salt and pepper and dredge through flour until it looks like a large marshmallow. Fry the meat in oil in a heavy pan until it's brown on both sides. Don't worry about overcooking the meat — the idea of chicken-fried steak is that the meat is overcooked. After you feel it can't be cooked any longer, remove the beef and stir whatever flour is left into the drippings in the pan. Add the milk. Stir and cook until the gravy is smooth, adding more milk if necessary. Pour over the steak. Listen as your arteries harden.

Serves One

"Frito" Pie

After the deprivations necessitated by World War II, Americans were happy to eat just about anything. This may explain the Fritos® Pie craze (yes, I know the world calls it "Frito Pie," but in print a trademark is a trademark and we damn well better respect it!) that swept the western states in the late forties. Of course, the marketing department of the Fritos Corn Chip Company also went into overtime once the war was over, convincing Americans that a bag of Fritos corn chips, topped with chili, grated cheddar cheese and onions, was a great dish. In its most basic form, the "pie" is created by ripping open the top of a bag of chips and pouring in canned chili. In situations like that, cheese and onions are rarely available; we're talking AM-PM Mini-Mart Cuisine here. In a more formal style, suitable for family meals, the pie can be made at home. This dish is a major guilty pleasure; it tastes far better than you want to admit it possibly could.

---

* **1 large bag Fritos corn chips**
* **1 can industrial-strength chili con carne**
* **1 chopped onion**
* **1 bag grated Cheddar**
* **cheese**
* **salsa**

Pour the corn chips into a pie pan, a baking pan or anything that will go into the oven. Heat the chili in a pan, then pour chili over corn chips, top with the onions, then lots of chili and, finally, the cheese. Spike with salsa if such is your desire. Place under the broiler for two or three minutes, until the cheese is melted and runny. Consume with beer.

Serves Two

Loco Moco

Though Hawaiian cuisine usually brings up images of luaus with kahlua pig and lomi lomi salmon, locals in the Hawaiians Islands prefer to think of their cooking as plate lunch, saimin . . . and the rather madcap late forties creation known as loco moco. The variations on this working-class combination of rice, hamburger, eggs and gravy are nearly infinite. Forget exotic preparations of ahi, ono or mahi mahi. To bring a tear to a Hawaiian's eye, mention loco moco and he or she will tell tales of where to find the best of the best and who makes the very best gravy around. Living room luaus had their heyday in the fifties. In the forties, however, Americans were already experiencing a deep appreciation for things Hawaiian, and returning servicemen as well as tourists brought this dish back to the mainland. This particular version is typical, if a bit better than most.

* **1 cup cooked white rice**
* **1 hamburger patty**
* **2 eggs**
* **1 teaspoon crushed garlic**
* **1 tablespoon soy sauce**
* **1/2 onion, chopped**
* **1 small can tomato sauce**
* **salt and pepper**

Begin by putting a layer of steamed rice on a plate. Top with a well-done hamburger patty. Fry two eggs and place atop the burger. In a small pot, combine the garlic, soy, onion, tomato sauce, salt and pepper to taste. Bring it to a boil, then pour it over the egg and burger. Eat while still very hot.

Serves One

The Mai Tai

In his lifetime, Trader Vic Bergeron claimed to have invented dozens of drinks. And no doubt he did, many of which live on not just at the various branches of Trader Vic's but in bars all over the world. In his definitive Trader Vic's Bartender's Guide, he describes the creation of what may be his finest beverage, which he knocked together in 1944 in honor of some friends visiting from Tahiti. Tasting the drink, which Trader Vic had made using 17-year-old rum, one of the friends complimented him, saying the drink was "Mai Tai," or "out of this world." The name stuck. And Trader Vic was so proud of being able to claim its invention, he ends his tale saying, "Anybody who says I didn't create this drink is a dirty stinker. The recipe according to Trader Vic:

---

* **1 lime**
* **1/2 ounce orange curacao**
* **1/4 ounce rock candy syrup**
* **1/4 ounce orgeat**
* **1 ounce dark Jamaica rum**
* **1 ounce Martinique rum**

Squeeze the lime juice over shaved ice in a double Old Fashioned glass. Add the remaining ingredients, stir and decorate with a slice of lime, mint and various fruit.

Serves One

Pepper Steak

As America returned to normalcy in the forties, it also returned to its national love of beef. Interestingly, two dishes called pepper steak began to appear on menus from coast to coast. One was really a peppercorn steak, in which a large chunk of beef, often a New York strip, was studded with cracked peppercorns, broiled, then dipped in peppercorns a second time so that the outside of the meat was virtually crusted with peppercorns both cooked and fresh — a fascinating combination of tastes and textures. The other pepper steak, offered here, was more of a stew, in which a less expensive cut of beef was cooked with a variety of peppers — a vaguely Italian dish that was a standard in American homes throughout the forties, fifties and well into the sixties.

---

* **1 small beef roast, cut into strips and cubes**
* **1/4 cup olive oil**
* **2 large sliced onions**
* **1 large can chopped tomatoes**
* **2 cups beef stock**
* **6 bell peppers, red and green, sliced into strips**
* **a bunch parsley**
* **salt and pepper**

Quickly braise the beef in olive oil in a large pot. Then add the onions, tomatoes and beef stock, cover tightly, and cook over a low heat for about half an hour. In a separate pan, saute the peppers in more olive oil. Add to the meat, and cook for 10 minutes more. Serve with rice or potatoes.

Serves Six

Philadelphia Cheesesteak

In the 1940s there was one reason to visit Philadelphia that had nothing to do with the Liberty Bell, and that was the Philadelphia cheesesteak sandwich served at Pat's King of Steaks at 1237 East Passyunk Avenue. In 1948 the folks at Pat's finally added cheese to the steak sandwich they'd been serving there for several decades. Soon the immensely popular sandwiches were being copied at fast food spots all over the country. And, as with most legendary eats, none were as good as the original. This is a dish that's difficult to replicate at home, but those who can't make it to Philly with any regularity might try the following for at least a taste (a small taste) of the real thing.

---

* **frozen steak, sliced very thin**
* **shredded American cheese (or mozzarella if you want to be avant-garde)**
* **sliced onions**
* **vegetable oil**
* **1 submarine sandwich roll**
* **shredded lettuce**
* **mayonnaise**
* **salt and pepper**

Quickly saute several slices of frozen beef in vegetable oil, seasoning with salt and pepper while they cook. Turn and cook till all redness vanishes, and set aside. Saute the onions in remaining juices till soft. Return the beef to the pan with the onions and add cheese. Cook till cheese is fully melted and well mixed with beef and onions. Fill the roll with lettuce, spread the mayo and pack in the beef, onion and cheese mixture. Eat.

Serves One

Spam and Beans

The name Spam comes from the "sp" in spicy and "am" in ham. Over the years, its maker, Hormel, has advertised Spam as "The Meat of Many Uses," "A Lot of Meals, But Not a Lot of Money" and "There's a World of Things You Can Do with Spam." Soldiers carried it all over the Pacific during the war, and it remains wildly popular in Hawaii and the South Pacific. In The Happy Isles of Oceania, *travel writer Paul Theroux suggests that its popularity in that region has some-thing to do with the locals' cannibalistic past.*

---

* ⋆ **2 16-ounce cans baked beans**
* ⋆ **1 medium onion, minced**
* ⋆ **4 tablespoons pickle relish**
* ⋆ **2 teaspoons mustard**
* ⋆ **1 7-ounce bottle 7-Up**
  (or Coke or Pepsi)
* ⋆ **1/3 cup molasses**
* ⋆ **1 tablespoon Worcestershire sauce**
* ⋆ **salt and pepper to taste**
* ⋆ **1 can Spam, diced**

Combine all of the ingredients except the Spam in a good-size casserole dish. Mix well. Top with the Spam cubes. Bake uncovered in a 325 degree oven for two hours.

Serves Eight

Ike and Onion Dip
1950~1960

It was a decade when people may have dressed seriously (the man in the gray flannel suit, the woman in the crinoline skirt), may have driven serious cars (the Cadillac, the Lincoln Continental, the Chevrolet Impala), may have lived in serious suburbs where they seriously practiced duck-and-cover drills in case A- and H-bombs were on their way from the enemies of democracy. Ike, a serious President, was in the White House. Dick, his terribly serious Vice President, was very busy making serious explanations for his illegal slush funds, seriously talking about his dog Checkers. It was a decade of conformity and straight-arrow life-styles — which makes me wonder why the culinary habits of the decade were so absolutely . . . zany.

In the history of twentieth-century cuisine, the fifties are unprecedented in their sheer whimsy. It was an age of living room luaus and tiki torches on the patio, of cheese balls and crepes suzettes, of duck a l'orange and moo goo gai pan, of baked Alaska and chocolate fondue, of barbecued bologna and tuna casserole, of tomato aspic and cocktail Spam, pickle pinwheels and sardine sandwiches, creamed eggplant on toast and blue cheese chicken. Beef Stroganoff was a big item in the fifties, with hamburger Stroganoff working just fine for those on a budget. It was the age of chicken divan, lobster thermidor and tournedos Rossini. The privations of the thirties and forties were at an end. Money flowed like water. And Americans had a ball at the dinner table.

It's not of small import that the TV dinner was born in the fifties. Although television had been functional for part of the forties, it wasn't until the fifties — the golden age of television — that the American neuron system was integrated forever with the boob tube. It was the decade of *Your Show of Shows, The Lone Ranger, Arthur Godfrey's Talent Scouts, Hopalong Cassidy, I Love Lucy, The Red Skelton Show, The Jack Benny Show, Dragnet, You Bet Your Life, The Life of Riley, The Jackie Gleason Show, The $64,000 Question, Disneyland, The Ed Sullivan Show, Gunsmoke, I've Got a Secret, Wagon Train, Father Knows Best, The Price Is Right* and *The Real McCoys*. Americans didn't want to ever be disconnected from their beloved television sets. In December 1953, C.A. Swanson & Sons of Omaha, Nebraska, introduced the frozen TV dinner. And the world changed forever.

It was a turkey dinner, costing ninety-eight cents for a sectioned aluminum tray that contained turkey ("Mostly White Meat"), dressing and gravy, peas (at first) or carrots (later, "in a seasoned sauce") and, in the beginning, sweet potatoes flavored with orange juice (later replaced with whipped white potatoes). In theory, at least, it was created as yet another labor-saving device for housewives.

It's interesting to note that nowhere on the package was the term "TV dinner" actually used. But when the Swanson Turkey Dinner came out in 1953, the parents of the baby boom generation immediately grasped the possibilities. The only cooking skill needed was the ability to turn on the oven and peel back some foil. Kids just loved the compartmentalized trays. Indeed, an entire semiotic developed over the proper form for consuming a TV dinner. Should one eat the dinner one compartment at a time, neatly and assiduously? Or should one combine the elements on one's fork in some symbolic manner? Compulsive that I am, I always consumed the dinners one item at a time, not moving on to the next until the previous had been finished. I also alphabetize my spices.

Though I'm rather fond of the concept of the TV dinner, there's little doubt that it struck a death knell for the grand old tradition of cooking at home. Add to the TV dinner the logarithmic expansion of McDonald's and Burger King and the dominance of Wonder Bread and its ilk, and cooking would seem to have been on the verge of extinction in America. And yet, it didn't disappear. It simply went through a reformation of sorts in which flavors became highly standardized. Regional boundaries between cuisine began to disappear. It was the beginning of the age when you

didn't have to travel cross country to buy a package of, say, Thomas' English Muffins or U-Bet Chocolate Syrup. As the decade evolved, these products began to appear everywhere — or, at least, everywhere in the big cities.

Various canned goods, instant foods and frozen products became the clarion call of the age. In 1950, the Green Giant Company was formed, with its ubiquitous symbol of the Jolly ("ho ho ho") Green Giant. That same year General Foods introduced Minute Rice, which cooked in a single minute instead of taking twenty minutes. It didn't taste as good as regular rice but it was good enough for those in a rush, especially for those who ate their rice topped with gravy made from a packaged mix while watching *The Milton Berle Show*.

Tropicana was born in 1951, saving Americans the inconvenience of having to squeeze their own orange juice. Pream came along in 1952 — no more having to run to the store for cream for your coffee. That same year the first diet soft drink, No-Cal Ginger Ale, was introduced. A modern-day miracle! Drink all the soda you want, and never gain an ounce! By 1953 there were fifteen thousand pizzerias in the country, with frozen pizzas available at thousands of markets — one more dinner that Americans didn't have to bother cooking. Special K breakfast cereal came along in 1955 — vitamins in your cereal.

In 1954 a milk shake machine salesman named Ray Kroc became fascinated with the fast-food concept the brothers Mac and Dick McDonald developed in the previous decade in San Bernardino, California, and asked them to sell him franchise rights. He opened his first branch a year later in Des Plaines, Illinois, near Chicago, charging fifteen cents for burgers and ten cents for fries. By 1959 he had opened a hundred outlets. It was, and still is, in many ways the singular apotheosis of the American culinary experience.

Consider the Big Mac (which actually made its debut in 1968, but it's utterly intrinsic to the Mickey D concept), a classic construction of thirteen layers, coincidentally (or perhaps not so coincidentally) the number of the original thirteen colonies and the number of stars on the original flag flown so proudly during the American Revolution. The layers are top bun, onions, meat, pickles, lettuce, Secret Sauce, middle bun, onions, meat, cheese, lettuce, Secret Sauce, bottom bun. The Secret Sauce is the perfect American topping, a Thousand Island-like mayonnaise-based dressing that's pleasantly sweet, somewhat orange and textured with bits of pickle relish. It's been observed that Americans will eat anything if it's orange and sweet. By that definition, Secret Sauce is the very essence of American taste.

Americans will also eat anything crunchy; it's been said that the most popular flavor in America is crispy. McDonald's French fries are crispy, almost definitively so; that time spent under heat lamps crisps them even more. In terms of service, McDonald's is Henry Ford's assembly line

reconfigured for food preparation. In terms of appearance, it's Hemingway's "clean, well-lighted place." McDonald's is America. More than the taut observation that what's good for General Motors is good for America, what's good for America is McDonald's, the culinary guiding light of the second half of the twentieth century.

McDonald's wasn't the only fast-food franchise to take the country by storm. Colonel Sanders hit the road in 1955 to sell his recipe to franchisees in return for 3 percent of their gross, and fried chicken in a box became an American institution. Pizza Hut opened in 1958, on its way to becoming a behemoth in the world of home pizza delivery.

Denny's was born in the fifties. So was the Diners Club Card, the first credit card, which was accepted at first at twenty-seven restaurants in the New York area. Dunkin' Donuts came into being, along with the first Holiday Inn. And in 1953, Kraft gave the world Cheese Whiz. Procter & Gamble gave us Jif peanut butter in 1958. Rice-a-Roni was born that same year. So was the International House of Pancakes. And so was the ice cream called Häagen-Dazs — an American creation with a Danish-sounding name that has no meaning in Danish at all.

The fifties were, simply speaking, the strangest culinary decade of the century. It was a time of remarkable formality — in dress, in manners, in dinner parties, at which chicken divan, beef

Stroganoff and lobster thermidor were the primary entrees. It was also a time of remarkable informality: the age of the dip, the backyard barbecue, the bridge party, the potluck.

By the fifties, Jell-O had become a central element in American cooking, appearing in salads as a sort of modern-day aspic and in a wide variety of desserts that went well beyond the simple Jell-O jiggle. There was cheesecake made with Jell-O (and a very good one, too), banana and sour cream mold, spicy cranberry-orange mold, Jell-O pumpkin pie . . . .

However, no culinary fad so totally epitomizes the fifties as the Great Swiss Fondue Panic that swept the nation. John Mariani pinpoints the beginning of the craze at New York's Swiss Chalet Restaurant, where, in 1956, chef and owner Konrad Egli introduced fondue Bourguignonne, a beef fondue that quickly became the rage. For most Americans, though, the fondue of choice was cheese.

Judging by our cuisine, we were trying to redefine ourselves during the fifties. And redefined we were. It was during the fifties that Julia Child finalized the recipes for *Mastering the Art of French Cooking*, which was published in 1961, a book that almost single-handedly returned us to reality. It brought us back to the kitchen at the beginning of a brand-new decade. ★

Onion Dip (a.k.a California Dip)

In 1952, the Lipton Food Company introduced a dehydrated onion soup mix that had limited success at first. Within a year, though, word began to spread on the California party circuit that the mix could be combined with sour cream at the ratio of two envelopes of mix to one cup of sour cream. The resulting remarkable dip came to be known as California Dip. It became so quickly popular that by 1953 Lipton was printing the recipe for the dip on its onion soup packages. The company says that to this day, more envelopes of onion soup mix are turned into dip than onion soup.

★ **2 envelopes of Lipton Onion Soup**

★ **1 cup sour cream**

Combine the above and serve with chips, crackers, celery . . . .

Serves a little crowd

Beef Stroganoff

Conventional wisdom would suggest that as a simple response to the Soviet menace — and to avoid the slightest taint of Communist involvement — Americans would have kept a considerable distance from any dish with Russian roots. And yet there was hardly a proper hostess of the time who didn't prepare beef Stroganoff in copious quantities. It was surprisingly easy to make — and remarkably high in cholesterol as well.

---

* **1 pound beef tenderloin tips**
* **1/2 cup butter**
* **1 cup peeled baby onions**
* **1 teaspoon minced garlic**
* **1/2 pound sliced mushrooms**
* **salt, pepper, nutmeg and paprika**
* **1 cup beef or chicken stock**
* **1 cup sour cream**

Thinly slice the beef, melt the butter in a skillet, and brown the beef in it. Remove the beef, and add the onions, garlic and mushrooms to the buttery juice. Saute until tender, then add the broth, bring to a boil, and return the beef to the skillet. Season with salt, pepper and a pinch of nutmeg. Turn down the heat, and carefully add the sour cream, being careful not to let it boil. Serve over egg noodles.

Serves Six

Fish Sticks

More than a few children of the fifties and sixties grow bilious and pale at even the mention of fish sticks. They find them oily and nasty, good only as an excuse for eating tartar sauce. It was in 1952 that Mrs. Paul's Kitchens began selling frozen fish sticks, freeing mothers across America from ever having to bother cooking again. With slightly mushy interiors and breading that tasted a bit like mashed cornflakes, fish sticks defined Friday evening dinners for a generation. It wasn't until the appearance of sushi years later that baby boomers came to accept the basic goodness of seafood. You can make your own fish sticks if you want to, though why you might want to is beyond me.

---

* **1 pound cod or halibut filets, cut into short strips**
* **1/2 cup milk**
* **1 cup bread crumbs**
* **1/4 cup melted butter**

Dip the fish pieces in milk, then in bread crumbs. Place on a lightly buttered pan and bake in a 350 degree oven until golden brown. Baste the fish with the melted butter occasionally. Turn once. Serve with tartar sauce.

Serves Four

Grasshopper Pie

Perhaps the most unique (and one of the most popular) Jell-O desserts ever, the mildly unbelievable grasshopper pie managed to combine lime Jell-O with green crème de menthe. It included Cool Whip for good measure.

Crust

* 1-1/2 cups crumbled chocolate cookies
* 1/4 cup melted butter

Filling

* 1 small package Lime Jell-O
* 2/3 cup hot water
* 1/2 cup cold water
* 2 tablespoons green crème de menthe
* 2 tablespoons white crème de cacao
* 1 cup Cool Whip

Combine the crumbled cookies and butter and press into a 9-inch pie pan.

Prepare the Jell-O according to the instructions on the box, but use 2/3 cup hot water and 1/2 cup cold water. As the Jell-O begins to solidify, mix the liqueurs into the Cool Whip, then whisk the Cool Whip into Jell-O. Chill slightly and spoon into the pie crust. Chill until firm.

Serves Six

The Piña Colada

What the Mai Tai did for rum in the forties, the Piña Colada did for rum in the fifties, satisfying Americans' continuing need to taste things Caribbean and to consume pineapple juice, coconut cream and Bacardi in unheard of quantities. The drink is claimed by a number of bars in San Juan, Puerto Rico, the most likely of which is the Caribe Hilton Hotel and Casino. Regardless of origin, the ultimate tropical drink began a craze that lasted for the rest of the century. So long-lived is the popularity of the Piña Colada that in 1979 singer Rupert Holmes hit with a number-one song titled "Escape (The Piña Colada Song)," in which he praises the power of a glassful of rum, pineapple juice and coconut cream.

---

* **2 ounces golden Puerto Rican rum**
* **3 ounces unsweetened pineapple juice**
* **1 ounce coconut cream**

Blend with crushed ice. Garnish with a chunk of pineapple and a maraschino cherry.

Serves One

Ike and Onion Dip

Russian Dressing

Along with beef Stroganoff, the American interest in things Russian led to a rebirth of Russian dressing. It had been around since the turn of the century but didn't really catch on until in the fifties, when it began to appear on deli sandwiches and on salads in the steakhouses of New York. Virtually overnight, Russian dressing (a cousin of Thousand Island dressing) became ubiquitous, the dressing to demand for those of discernment and taste. It held on for at least a decade, eventually eclipsed by a two-sided attack from vinaigrette and blue cheese dressings.

---

1 cup mayonnaise

1/4 cup chili sauce

1/4 cup ketchup

1 teaspoon chopped scallions

1 teaspoon pickle relish

Combine all ingredients. Serve over mixed greens.

Serves Six

The Screwdriver

Very probably the libation that inebriated more teens in the fifties than any other, this appealing mixture of orange juice and vodka was, and is, a marvel when it comes to disguising both the taste and the aroma of alcohol. Vodka, which is almost tasteless, is cleverly hidden by the sweetness of the orange juice. Thanks to a number of brands of premixed Screwdrivers, nothing was needed to get a buzz on but the ability to unscrew a top. Making a Screwdriver is a total no-brainer as well. This is just as well, for after more than a couple, no brains are about all that's left.

1-1/2 ounces vodka

3 ounces orange juice

Mix over ice. Drink.

Serves One

Sloppy Joe

While proper America dreamed of cheese fondue and beef Stroganoff, working-class America was having a fine time with a Midwestern favorite that seems to have appeared on the scene as a way of stretching expensive protein during World War II and grew in popularity during the fifties to the point that it briefly rivaled the hamburger, meat loaf and chili as America's favorite way of eating ground beef.

* **1 pound ground beef**
* **cooking oil**
* **1/2 cup chopped onions**
* **1/4 cup chopped green peppers**
* **1/4 cup condensed tomato soup**
* **1/4 cup ketchup**
* **garlic salt to taste**
* **salt and pepper to taste**
* **hamburger buns**

Saute the beef in oil in the skillet until brown. Add the onions and peppers, tomato soup and ketchup, salt and pepper. Cook until very well done, about half an hour. Add garlic salt if desired. A healthy dash of Tabasco doesn't hurt either. Serve on nice soft hamburger buns.

Serves Four

Cheese Fondue

During the Great Swiss Fondue Panic, almost any fondue would do. But most Americans served cheese fondue in those little fondue pots in tones of harvest gold and avocado. Interestingly, cheese fondue continued the necessity for kirsch begun with cherries jubilee; fans of global conspiracy theories tend to see the hand of the kirsch makers behind far too many of our national dining habits.

---

* **1 tablespoon olive oil**
* **1 crushed clove garlic**
* **1 pound good Swiss cheese (Gruyere, Emmentaler, raclette)**
* **2 tablespoons flour**
* **1 cup slightly sweet white wine (Johannisberg riesling works well)**
* **1/4 cup kirsch**
* **pinch nutmeg**
* **salt and pepper to taste**
* **1 loaf French or Italian bread, cubed and toasted**

Moisten the inside of the fondue pot with olive oil, and rub it with the crushed garlic clove to impart some flavor. Grate the cheese and mix it with the flour. Add the wine to the pot and begin warming. Add the cheese and stir while it melts. Add the kirsch, nutmeg, salt and pepper to taste. Spear cubes of bread with fondue forks and dip them into the resulting goo.

Serves Eight

Tuna Noodle Casserole

Along with fish sticks, one of the classics of home cuisine in the fifties was tuna noodle casserole, a ubiquitous dish with dozens of permutations, some made with cream of mushroom soup, some with cream of celery soup. In their book Square Meals, Jane and Michael Stern even identify a tuna noodle casserole topped with crumbled Ritz Crackers. No one who grew up in the fifties was denied the dubious pleasures of this oddly satisfying dish. Indeed, at a foods-of-your-childhood party I threw some years ago, one-third of the guests brought tuna noodle casseroles. It felt more like a religious totem than something to eat on Wednesday night.

---

* **1 can Campbell's Cream of Celery or Cream of Mushroom Soup**
* **1/2 cup milk**
* **1 cup peas**
* **1 can onion rings**
* **2 7-ounce cans tuna, drained**
* **2 cups cooked egg noodles**
* **1/2 cup shredded Cheddar cheese**

Mix the soup with the milk, peas, tuna, onion rings and noodles. Bake in a 400 degree oven for thirty minutes. Top with the shredded cheese and bake until the cheese melts and browns.

Serves Four

Cooking for Camelot and Aquarius 1960-1970

In the sixties, many Americans rediscovered French cooking, in part thanks to Julia Child and in part thanks to Jacqueline Kennedy. They pulled back a country that hovered on a culinary abyss. Had it not been for their combined efforts, Americans might have gotten too busy to cook altogether.

Social critics of the time filled volumes complaining about the near extinction of the family meal — the life-style displayed on *Father Knows Best* was viewed as nothing more than a mildly nostalgic myth. America was a nation on the go, and we ate most of our meals on the run, grabbing a bite here and there when we could. After decades of growth, the fast-food restaurant and the frozen meal reached their apotheoses. Frozen food, convenience food, instant food were all terms of endearment rather than the terms of disparagement they later became.

Julia kicked off the decade with the 1961 publication of *Mastering the Art of French Cooking*. Jackie hired a master French chef to prepare state dinners at the White House. At the White House, guests ate poulet chasseur and framboises à la crème chantilly.

Despite their efforts, many home cooks, including my own mother, would not be rescued. (Back then, my mother made a rather strange dish that began with a thick hamburger patty, dropped still frozen into the bottom of what my mother referred to as a "waterless pot," on top of which she sprinkled a bagful of Tater Tots doused with ketchup.) Cooks such as my mother had become so enamored with convenience foods, they cooked virtually nothing from scratch. Swanson's Frozen Chicken Pot Pie, Potato Buds instant mashed potatoes and every manner of frozen vegetables were standard fare. It seemed as though no one I knew bought fresh vegetables in the sixties. Or, at least, it seemed to be true for the first half of the decade.

Then, sometime around 1967, we stopped getting our hair cut, stopped wearing ties and started using words like *organic*, *natural* and *pure*. The pendulum did some serious swinging. After making nothing in the first years of the decade, a great contingent of Americans started making everything possible — as long as it was in tune with the universe. Freshly baked bread could be smelled on every street in the Haight-Ashbury of San Francisco, the East Village of New York and Los Angeles' Laurel Canyon. Well, you could sort of smell it after you got past the pungent aroma of marijuana. The bread was used to make sandwiches of homemade peanut butter, homegrown bean sprouts, home-mashed tahini and hummus. It was as though we were going through a national cleansing, of the spirit and of the palate. No doubt it was much needed.

As Elspeth Huxley wrote in her book *Brave New Victuals* in 1965, "We are eating too much of some things, notably sugar. Nutritionally speaking sugar is little more than potted energy. Of course we need energy, but less of it than we did, now that fewer of us are employed in hewing coal, wielding picks, humping sacks or scrubbing floors, and more in sitting still, and therefore should be eating foods with fewer calories, and more vitamins and proteins . . . Today we eat in a fortnight as much sugar as our ancestors, a couple of centuries back, ate in a year." Or as the wonderfully acerbic John and Karen Hess wrote in *The Taste of America* a few years later, "We have become a bastion of sugar addicts. We give our babies a formula that provides something like two teaspoons of sugar per feeding, wean them on heavily sweetened baby foods, and raise them on double-sweetened frankfurter and hamburger buns, sweet ketchup, candy and drinks. We consume more of this poor nutrient than any society ever has, and we look for it in everything we eat — bread, meat, even soups, vegetables and salads."

By the sixties, we had become a society that, to paraphrase E.W. Howe, ate as if we were fattening ourselves up for the market. And so many of us went the other way, inspiring Fran Lebowitz to observe later that "thoroughly distasteful as synthetic foods might be, one cannot help but accord them a certain value when confronted with the health food buff. Brown rice is ponderous, overly chewy, and possessed of unpleasant religious overtones."

We had turned from a nation in which the rich ate like pashas and the poor subsisted on what they could to a nation in which almost everyone ate well. But just what constituted "well" wasn't well defined. In the early years of the century, it was roasted beef and poultry, a lobster or two, a smattering of vegetables and lots of cream and butter sauces. By the sixties, the phenomenon known as *nostalgie de la boue* — "nostalgia for the mud" — had set in. Folks who could afford to live on nothing but caviar and truffles, and white truffles at that, opted instead to spend their days in unheated tepees gnawing on brown rice flavored with some seaweed. The vegetarian casserole become the standard for a whole generation of otherwise upwardly mobile citizens, who proudly sliced and diced broccoli and tofu and called it food.

Thankfully, not everyone went the way of no flesh. For the rest of America, though defrosting might have been the main form of cooking during the week, the cuisine of choice at dinner parties was that which had been handed down on a whole book full of tablets by Julia. She taught us the virtues of tossing things about the kitchen, taking nothing too seriously and cooking coq au vin and boeuf Bourguignon for every occasion — dishes that only the

most craven of fools could possibly ruin. Julia's culinary secrets were simple — use lots of eggs, butter, cream and flour and always have a good time doing it. She returned us to the days of duck à l'orange, steak au poivre and veal Orloff, all served with green beans amandine. She kept us sane in an era that was half sugar shock and half intestinal constriction.

In 1960, a 23-year-old entrepreneur named Thomas Monaghan opened the first branch of a pizza delivery chain called Domino's. The year 1961 gave us Frito-Lay, the quintessential chip and dip company — the result of a merger between the H.W. Lay Company and Frito — along with Coffee-Mate non-dairy creamer and Total breakfast cereal (gotta get those vitamins). Diet-Rite came along in 1962, along with aluminum cans with tab openers. Tab followed closely in 1963. So did Weight Watchers — and about time. By the early sixties, more than half of all adults qualified as overweight, and half of those were what the medical profession politely referred to as seriously obese.

In 1964, Kellogg introduced Pop-Tarts, an intriguing irony for a company started by a health food fanatic. General Foods gave us Awake synthetic orange juice, and General Mills gave us Lucky Charms, which fostered the fascinating proposition that freeze-dried marshmallows were an appropriate breakfast food. As the decade spread out, we were introduced to Diet Pepsi and Apple Jacks breakfast cereal in 1965, Bac-Os in 1966, the first home microwave ovens in 1967, the Big Mac in 1968, and Pringles — artificially fabricated potato chips — in 1969. In retrospect, it's no surprise millions turned to brown rice and tofu, which may not have tasted very good but could at least be identified as something akin to real food. In the sixties, baby boomers began graduating from college and were soon eating more of their meals out of the house than in it — an unprecedented phenomenon. ★

Banana Bread

It was as if an alien ray struck America from coast to coast. Suddenly, in the early sixties, everyone started baking banana bread. It was the strangest darned thing. After all, recipes for banana bread had been around for most of the century. And bananas, unlike kiwifruit, weren't exactly new. What seems to have happened is that America rediscovered the joys of baking. While most breads required a certain level of skill, banana bread (which is really more of a cake than a bread) was a cinch. There was no yeast to deal with, no rising and kneading, nothing but a sweet, rather moist, cake-bread that tasted great with cream cheese on it and proved that the maker was one with his or her kitchen.

---

* ★ **2 eggs**
* ★ **1/2 cup vegetable oil**
* ★ **1/2 cup sugar**
* ★ **1/2 cup honey**
* ★ **1 tablespoon lemon juice**
* ★ **1 tablespoons buttermilk**
* ★ **1 tablespoon yogurt**
* ★ **2 cups very ripe mashed bananas**
* ★ **2 cups all-purpose flour**
* ★ **1/4 teaspoon cinnamon**
* ★ **1/4 teaspoon nutmeg**
* ★ **1/2 teaspoon salt**
* ★ **1/2 teaspoon baking soda**
* ★ **1 cup chopped nuts**

Combine the eggs, oil, sugar, honey, lemon juice, buttermilk, yogurt and bananas. Beat until smooth. Work in the flour, cinnamon, nutmeg, salt and baking soda. Fold in the nuts. Bake in an oiled loaf pan at 350 degrees for thirty minutes, then lower the heat to 325 degrees for thirty minutes more.

Serves Eight

Fettuccine Alfredo

Americans traveling to Italy returned with tales of a remarkable pasta concoction

that put the old standby of spaghetti and meatballs to shame. It was found at

Ristorante Alfredo alla Scrofa in Rome, known there at first as fettuccine al triplo

burro — *fettuccine with three butters. It came to be known as fettuccine Alfredo*

and, in its own way, did as much to introduce the non-red-sauce cooking of

Northern Italy as any dish. It also did more than its fair share to raise cholesterol

levels and add inches around the waist.

---

* **1 pound fettuccine**
* **1/2 cup sweet butter**
* **2 egg yolks**
* **1 cup cream**
* **1/2 teaspoon nutmeg**
* **white pepper to taste**
* **1 cup freshly grated**
  Parmesan cheese

While the pasta cooks, beat the two egg yolks with a spoonful of the cream. Warm the remainder of the cream over a low flame, and beat in the cream and egg yolk mixture, whipping for about five minutes. Add nutmeg, salt and white pepper to taste. When the pasta is done, strain and return to pot. Cut butter into small chunks, and melt in still-hot pasta. Add half the parmesan and the cream and egg mixture, and toss until well coated. Sprinkle on remaining cheese and serve, flavoring with more salt and pepper if needed.

Serves Four

Gazpacho

By the mid-sixties, no proper outdoor party was without the classic cold Spanish soup known as gazpacho, which smacked of a pleasant ethnic exoticism. It comes in dozens of forms in Spain, but its American incarnation was basically uniform — a sort of V-8 with texture that was easy to make, tasted great and had almost no calories at all.

---

* ★ 6 large ripe tomatoes, peeled and chopped
* ★ 1 medium onion
* ★ 3 scallions
* ★ 2 cloves garlic
* ★ 1 cucumber, peeled and chopped
* ★ 1 green bell pepper, sliced
* ★ 1 red bell pepper
* ★ 1/4 cup olive oil
* ★ 2 tablespoons red wine vinegar
* ★ 2 tablespoons lemon juice
* ★ salt and pepper to taste
* ★ 1/4 cup mixed dried parsley, basil and thyme

Peel and chop the tomatoes. Chop together the onion, scallions and garlic. Mix with the tomatoes. Put the chopped vegetables into an electric blender. Add the olive oil, vinegar, lemon juice, salt and pepper. Blend on high until mostly liquid but with enough texture to keep it interesting. Serve in individual cups, sprinkled with the herb mixture.

Serves Four

Guacamole

The sixties saw an explosion of Mexican, or at least Tex-Mex, restaurants from coast to coast. What had formerly been a cuisine limited to the Southwest and the West Coast suddenly turned into a cooking style popular in Chicago, New York, Boston and Miami. Words like taco, enchilada *and* burrito *were no longer foreign. And almost universally loved was the addictive tortilla chip dip called guacamole, which any fool can make but very few make well.*

---

* **2 large ripe Haas avocados (Fuerte will do if Haas aren't available)**
* **1/2 chopped onion**
* **1 finely chopped garlic clove**
* **1 tablespoon lime juice (lemon juice will also do)**
* **1 teaspoon chile powder**
* **1 tablespoon La Victoria salsa (or other brand if not available)**

Slice the avocados in half, remove the pits and spoon the pulp into a bowl. Mash until smooth yet chunky. Add the onion, garlic, lime juice, chile powder and salsa. Work in without undermining the pleasant chunkiness of freshly made guacamole. Serve with tortilla chips and Margaritas.

Serves Four

Hash Brownies

The sixties were a time when legions of young adults often consulted The Alice B. Toklas Cookbook *for interesting recipes such as "haschisch fudge," which didn't call for any chocolate at all. For some reason, an actual chocolate treat, hash brownies — which for the sake of historical accuracy called for a bunch of hash or marijuana, pulverized in a blender — didn't make it into the Toklas cookbook. Just for the record the following recipe tastes just fine without any drugs at all.*

---

* ★ **1 cup butter**
* ★ **2 cups sugar**
* ★ **2 cups all purpose flour**
* ★ **2-1/2 cups milk**
* ★ **3 large eggs**
* ★ **3 ounces bittersweet chocolate**
* ★ **1/2 cup chopped pecans**

Melt the butter and mix in the sugar. Add the flour, milk and eggs, and beat until smooth and creamy. Melt the chocolate, blend in and then mix in the pecans. (Again, for the historical record, this is where those hippies added hallucinogens). Spread evenly in an oiled 9x13-inch baking pan. Bake at 300 degrees for forty minutes, or until done. Top with commercial frosting from a can, which tastes as good as the real thing and doesn't make a mess of your kitchen.

Makes 24 Brownies

Irish Coffee

If not the definitive drink of the sixties, then darned close — Irish coffee is a brilliant combination of Irish whiskey and coffee discovered in the early fifties at Ireland's Shannon Airport by San Francisco travel writer Stanton Delaplane, who carried the recipe back to the Buena Vista Cafe near the city's Fisherman's Wharf. By the sixties, the drink had become San Francisco's most popular libation and from there spread across the country.

---

* **2 sugar cubes**
* **1-1/2 ounces good Irish whiskey**
* **4 ounces coffee, hot and strong**
* **2 ounces heavy cream**

Warm a goblet with hot water so as not to shock the whiskey. Drop in the sugar cubes, pour the whiskey over them, then pour in the coffee. Whip the cream and spoon on top.

Serves One

Organic Mushroom Spread and Dip

By the late sixties, several million baby boomers were wearing Indian fabrics (both American Indian and Asian Indian) and had forsaken meat for bean sprouts and lentils. They were hippies, hippie camp followers, hippie wanna-bes and just plain folks who thought it would be groovy to do things in a natural, holistic, one-with-nature way. Of the many dishes popular in that period, only a few remain. One of my favorites is this terrific combination spread and dip made with mushrooms, various vegetables and, thank goodness, real mayonnaise (not the low-fat, no-fat stuff).

* 2 tablespoons olive oil
* 1 cup chopped mushrooms
* 1 teaspoon minced garlic
* 1/4 cup chopped red and green bell peppers
* 1/4 cup chopped scallions
* 1 teaspoon chopped fresh thyme
* 1 teaspoon chopped fresh parsley
* 1 teaspoon chopped fresh chervil
* 2 tablespoons lemon juice
* 1/4 cup mayonnaise
* salt, pepper and paprika

Briefly saute the mushrooms and garlic in the oil. Mix with the peppers, scallions, herbs, lemon juice and mayonnaise. Correct the seasoning, and top with paprika for color and flavor. Serve with crackers.

Serves Six

Nachos

Nachos have been around at least since the 1940s in the American southwest, and very possibly earlier than that. In the sixties, however, the dish became a standard at hundreds of Tex-Mex restaurants, where it was almost always ordered at the same time as the Margaritas and the guacamole (the guac used to make the nachos isn't enough to feed a gerbil! The more guac the merrier!). When made well, nachos are a perfect blend of crunchy and soft, spicy and mild, even hot and cold. And they're open to a world of individual interpretation.

---

* **1 package tortilla chips**
* **1/2 cup refried beans**
* **cooked chicken or beef if you wish**
* **8 ounces shredded cheese (mixed Monterey Jack and Cheddar work very well together)**
* **1/2 cup sliced jalapeños**
* **1/2 cup La Victoria salsa (or equivalent)**
* **1/2 cup sour cream**
* **1/2 cup guacamole**

On an oven-proof platter, layer the chips on the bottom, cover with the refried beans, the chicken or beef if you're using it and the salsa, and top with the cheese. Place under a broiler for two or three minutes, until the cheese is melted. Scatter the melted cheese with jalapeños, sour cream and guacamole.

Serves Four

Scampi

Scampi went through an interesting change in the sixties. Before then, the name referred to frozen shrimp of medium size, cooked with garlic, butter and lemon juice. But in the sixties, the actual scampi, which is a crustacean considerably larger than a shrimp and looks if anything more like a crayfish, began to appear on menus at better restaurants. During the sixties, this was one of the prime dishes served in upscale Italian/Continental restaurants. It eventually trickled down to garden-variety pasta places, where it was offered as a specialty of the house. Inevitably, these restaurants used smaller shrimp rather than the true, far larger scampi.

---

* **1 pound of the largest shrimp you can find**
* **1 tablespoon minced garlic**
* **1/4 pound butter**
* **2 tablespoons lemon juice**
* **1/4 cup dry white wine**
* **minced parsley**
* **cooked rice**
* **salt and pepper to taste**

Clean the shrimp. In a hot pan, melt the butter and saute the garlic. Just as the garlic begins to brown, toss in the shrimp and saute them on both sides until they're no longer translucent. Remove the shrimp from the pan and hold in serving dish. Add the lemon juice and white wine to the butter and garlic. Bring to a boil. Add several pinches of parsley. Pour over the shrimp. Then spoon the shrimp over rice.

Serves Two

Thousand Island Dressing

Crudités made a reappearance in the sixties and, along with them, came this cousin of Russian Dressing, which dates back to the early years of the century. The calorie-intensive dressing neatly canceled out the health benefits of the celery and carrot sticks.

* **1 cup mayonnaise**
* **1/4 cup chili sauce**
* **1/4 cup ketchup**
* **3 tablespoons chopped pickle relish**
* **1 green bell pepper, chopped**
* **1 scallion, chopped**
* **2 hard-cooked eggs, chopped**
* **pinch paprika**
* **salt and pepper**

Mix all ingredients well in a bowl. Serve on the side, remembering that the flavor will overwhelm most salads.

Serves Six

Mr. Wallbanger Goes to Brunch
1970~1980

If memory serves me right, America spent most of the seventies wearing platform shoes, designer jeans, Nik Nik shirts, wide-lapels, lots of polyester and some really overgrown sideburns. It was the decade of brunch, an age that seems really sort of . . . uncomfortable in retrospect. It was an age of surf 'n' turf, of beef 'n' brew, of heading for a salad bar as large as a trough. It was the decade when restaurants turned into events — the beginning of the concept of the restaurant as theatre. And when dining at home was a terribly confused time, raging between instant and frozen, and natural and organic. I don't think that as a nation we knew where we were going. And how could we have? Gerald Ford was in the White House, followed shortly thereafter by Jimmy Carter. A putter was followed by peanut butter.

It was a decade when anything went — one night you might be hanging out at a singles bar, drinking Harvey Wallbangers and eating cheeseburgers topped with Monterey Jack, the next night you'd be ensconced in a natural foods joint sucking down a broccoli and cheese casserole. If anything can be said for the seventies, it was the decade when ethnic restaurants really came into their own. And especially Asian cooking, which had been formerly limited to Chinese-American eateries with orchidaceous names like Blossom Garden, Pearl Palace and the Peking Panda. As the

'70s rolled along, we suddenly discovered the remarkable joys of the spicy cooking of Szechuan and Hunan, the deceptively simple pleasures of dim sum, and the awesome delights of that uncooked bit of culinary elegance called sushi.

It was as if the Great Cultural Revolution had leaped the Pacific, and in a transmogrified form was marching across tables in the Chinese restaurants of America.

Beginning in the late sixties, if a Chinese restaurant wanted to succeed in New York, it had to use the word *Szechuan* in its name — Szechuan Inn, Szechuan Garden, Szechuan Palace, 3-4-5 Szechuan, Szechuan Balcony, Szechuan Taste, Szechuan Kitchen. The food of choice was the hot, chili-flavored, smoked cooking of Szechuan, a barbarous province where the weather is colder than sin and pepper is virtually a religious sacrament. The measure of any Szechuan restaurant's stature was smoked duck — duck marinated overnight in ginger, orange peel, coriander, cinnamon and peppercorns that's steamed, then smoked over an aromatic fire of camphor wood and tea leaves. It was often served with spiced bean curd, eggplant sauteed in a peppery, fish-flavored sauce and peppery dumplings.

It took about half of the seventies for the Szechuan cooking of New York to make its way to San Francisco, where exactly the same phenomenon occurred — every restaurateur who wanted to stay in business changed the name of his establishment to Szechuan this or that and tossed handfuls of peppers into every dish. In more than a few cases, the cooking that resulted wasn't Szechuan at all; it was Chinese-American with a lot of peppers. It was Szechuan-American, which tended to be hot for hot's sake.

And speaking of hot, it was in the seventies that a small storefront restaurant opened in San Francisco called, simply, Hunan. In a bit of journalistic perversity, a column in *The New Yorker* named it the best Chinese restaurant in America. Soon after, there were lines down the block. Soon after that, Hunan restaurants started appearing all over New York, in many cases replacing the Szechuan places. Watchers of the scene often noticed that nothing changed except the name — if a dish had been called Szechuan beef, it was now Hunan beef. Same dish, different name. We were so obsessed with being on the cutting edge of Chinese food in the seventies that we absolutely had to be eating the cuisine of the moment, even if it wasn't.

By the end of the decade, big-city Americans had become downright Asia-philic. Thai restaurants appeared in many neighborhoods, especially in the Pacific Rim cities of the West Coast. Vietnamese and Korean cooking moved into the mainstream — or reasonably close to it. And a thing called sushi began to obsess foodies from coast to coast.

The first rash of sushi bars seems to have popped up in downtown San Francisco, starting in the mid-seventies to cater to visiting Japanese businessmen. To their owners' surprise, these places also attracted a wide demographic of diners, especially health-conscious yuppies who were up to their keesters in brown rice and bean sprouts and wanted something healthy, high in protein and low in fat that actually tasted good. Sushi was clearly the answer. It also offered the added edge of being a bit esoteric. The well-educated baby boomer knew that the way to approach sushi was to establish a relationship with the chef, to buy him beer, to drink much sake, to create obscure and often foolish rolls and in the end to pay through the nose for the experience. To be well versed in the ways of sushi was to be an American samurai, ready for life on the street.

It was a great time for ethnic eateries in general. Italian restaurants moved slowly from generic Italian to northern and southern Italian to deeply drawn lines of regional cuisine. Suddenly there were those that specialized in the cooking of Tuscany, Abruzzi, Venice, Milan, the Lake District, Apulia.

In the late seventies the British food press coined the word *foodie*, which it further explicated with the slogan: "Be Modern — Worship Food." Many did. Many still do.

There was much to make foodies

ecstatic. In 1971, Alice Waters, a French cultural studies major at the University of California, opened Chez Panisse in Berkeley, which may well have been the single most influential restaurant in America, or at least in California. It gave birth to the notion of California cuisine — intrinsically light cooking built around the bounty of California agriculture and aquaculture. In 1972, Le Perroquet opened in Chicago, proving that not all the good food was on the right and left coasts. In 1973, the critical team of Gault and Millau coined the term *nouvelle cuisine* in an article in their eponymous French magazine and, in the process, defined one of the culinary trends of the next decade and a half.

Home cooking ranged from instant and frozen to natural and organic. While the foodie sought out obscure greens and little known goat cheeses, even normal folks created odd dishes like granola fondue, lobster-asparagus mousse and a heck of a lot of quiche.

In the eighties we were told that real men don't consume quiche — an adage inspired by the seventies' fad for quiche. Everyone seemed to have a recipe for quiche, all sorts of quiche: crab or shrimp or spinach or zucchini or green tomato or even the classic quiche Lorraine. Especially popular was any recipe that didn't use nasty ingredients like bacon.

It was also a big decade for Crock-Pot cooking, a sort of fail-safe kitchen implement that came with a book full of dreadful recipes that involved pouring onion soup mix, cream of mushroom soup and a chicken into the pot, covering it and letting it cook all day. I remember making a horrifying dip in the Crock-Pot by dumping in bars of Velveeta, bottles of salsa and jars of jalapeños. I think the stuff could cook for all eternity without burning — or tasting like anything but hot sludge.

It was a big decade for beverage developments. The first light beer, Miller Lite, was introduced — seemingly striking a death knell to the hope that one day Americans would come to appreciate real beer. Perrier was introduced to the American market in 1976 and was an immediate hit with legions of Francophiles who firmly believed that not only was French cooking superior, so was their water.

For the first time, vodka outsold whiskey, very possibly because whiskey could be smelled on your breath and vodka couldn't; it was the Stealth bomber of alcoholic beverages. It was also the decade that the Eagles sang about a Tequila Sunrise and made it one of the most popular drinks in America, increasing tequila sales tenfold in the process. By the end of the seventies, Americans were also drinking more soft drinks than coffee or milk.

Our appetite for beef was bigger than ever. We ate a record-setting 128.5 pounds per person in 1976 (up from 85.1 pounds in 1960). However, by the end of the decade, at a longevity center in Santa Monica, people with heart disease were trying Nathan Pritikin's recommended regimen of very low-fat, low-cholesterol food combined with exercise. Change of every kind was in the wind. ★

The Harvey Wallbanger

The story, no doubt apocryphal, has this favorite invented at Pancho's Bar in Manhattan Beach, California, just south of Los Angeles. It's supposedly named for a surfer named Harvey, who consumed too many after a tournament and proceeded to . . . bang into walls. I've never met a surfer named Harvey. Nor have I ever met a surfer who would think to make a cocktail using Galliano. Still, the bar scene in the seventies was fueled on many levels by the Harvey Wallbanger. And its fans are right about one thing — drink too many, and you will bang into walls.

---

* **2 ounces vodka**
* **1/2 tablespoon Galliano liqueur**
* **4 ounces orange juice**

Shake with ice. Serve over ice cubes. Drink with care.

Serves One

Buffalo Chicken Wings

The dish was invented at the Anchor Bar in Buffalo, New York, on October 30, 1964, by owner Teressa Bellissimo in response to a supply of chicken wings sent to her husband, Frank (who had ordered backs and necks for his spaghetti sauce). The spicy deep-fried bar snack went on to become one of the definitive snack foods of the seventies and eighties. The dish does offer some bits of confusion, for the hot sauce-drenched wings (cut into pieces known as drummettes) are often served with celery sticks and blue-cheese dressing. Is the celery to be dipped in the dressing? Is the dressing for the wings? And if it's anything less than extremely hot, is it a real Buffalo chicken wing?

---

* 3 pounds chicken wings, the tips cut off and the remainder cut into drummettes
* 1/4 cup butter
* 1/2 cup hot sauce (Durkee Red Hot Sauce is usually called for)
* 1 tablespoon vinegar
* oil for deep frying
* 2 ounces crumbled blue cheese
* 1/2 cup mayonnaise
* 1/2 cup sour cream
* 1 bunch celery

In a saucepan, melt the butter and mix in the hot sauce and vinegar. Keep on low heat.

Heat the oil in a large, heavy pan and deep-fry the wings until they're brown. Drain them on paper towels, then toss in the saucepan with butter and hot sauce mix until they're well coated.

Combine the blue cheese, mayonnaise and sour cream in a blender until smooth. Trim the celery and separate into stalks. Serve the wings on one plate, the celery and blue cheese dressing on another. Wash down with lots of beer.

Serves Four

Eggs Benedict

Every Sunday, like lemmings heading for the sea, urbanites trekked to their local

fern bar and hotel restaurant to consume awesome quantities of Mimosas, Ramos

Fizzes and eggs Benedict. Though the dish dates back to the nineteenth century,

with claims to its origin going to both Delmonico's and the Waldorf-Astoria

(I'm rather fond of the idea of eggs Benedict as a hangover cure), it didn't really

take on a life of its own until the seventies, when it became the sine qua non of

brunch dishes. It also became a dish seriously abused by more than a few

restaurants; eggs Benedict served on a steam table is not to be tolerated.

---

* ★ **2 English muffins**
* ★ **4 slices Canadian bacon**
* ★ **4 eggs**
* ★ **butter as needed**

Split the muffins and toast them till lightly browned. Butter the muffins and arrange two halves on each plate. Saute the bacon in butter, and place one slice on each muffin half. Poach the eggs in boiling water for about four minutes, remove with a slotted spoon, and place one egg atop each bacon slice.

Hollandaise Sauce

* ★ **1/2 cup sweet butter**
* ★ **3 egg yolks**
* ★ **1 tablespoon lemon juice**

To make the sauce, let the butter melt in a double boiler while whisking the egg yolks and lemon juice together in a bowl. Pour yolks and lemon into butter, and stir constantly until smooth. Be careful not to overcook, for hollandaise sauce curdles easily. Pour over eggs.

Serves Two

Eggs Florentine

Even hard-core brunchers can eat only so many eggs Benedict. Omelets were ubiquitous but seemed somewhat plebeian in comparison. And so a wide realm of other egg dishes began to appear. Eggs Sardou (Benedict with artichoke hearts, ham, anchovies and truffles) and eggs Hussard (Sardou with grilled ham and marchand de vin sauce), though good, were even richer than eggs Benedict; after eating them for breakfast, passing the rest of the day in a coma was not unusual. But eggs Florentine, an American creation little known in Florence, has the virtue of seeming healthy because of its liberal use of spinach. Americans are rather sentimental when it comes to spinach, feeling that if it was good enough for Popeye, it must be great stuff. And as it's used in eggs Florentine, it is.

---

* **1 package frozen chopped spinach**
* **2 tablespoons butter**
* **1/2 teaspoon nutmeg**
* **8 eggs**

Cook the spinach and drain very well (nothing is more unpleasant than waterlogged eggs Florentine). Melt the butter, add the nutmeg, and mix with spinach. Arrange in the bottom of a casserole. Poach the eggs and carefully arrange atop the spinach.

Florentine Sauce

* **2 tablespoons butter**
* **2 tablespoons flour**
* **1 cup milk**
* **3 tablespoons cream**
* **1/4 cup grated Parmesan cheese**
* **salt and pepper to taste**

Make the sauce by melting the butter, mixing in the flour and slowly stirring in the milk until smooth. Add the cream and Parmesan cheese and season with salt and pepper. Pour over the spinach and eggs and quickly brown under the broiler.

Serves Four

Carrot Cake

In much the same way that banana bread became a standard virtually overnight in the sixties, carrot cake became the dessert of the 1970s. Because it was made with carrots, it was perceived as being healthy and low in calories. It is not, especially after you layer on the frosting. But it sure does taste good.

Cake

* ★ 3/4 cup vegetable oil
* ★ 1 cup sugar
* ★ 1 cup honey
* ★ 8 well-grated, peeled carrots
* ★ 2 cups all-purpose flour
* ★ 1 tablespoon baking powder
* ★ 1 teaspoon nutmeg
* ★ 1/2 teaspoon cinnamon
* ★ 1/2 teaspoon allspice
* ★ pinch salt
* ★ 4 eggs

Frosting

* ★ 2 8-ounce packages of cream cheese, softened
* ★ 1/4 cup sugar (or honey, as you wish)
* ★ 1-1/2 teaspoons vanilla

Mix all ingredients in a bowl. Pour into an oiled 9x13-inch cake pan. Bake at 350 degrees for 45 minutes to an hour, or until an inserted toothpick comes out clean. Cool the cake, remove from the pan and cover with the frosting.

To make the frosting, mash all ingredients in a bowl, then whip until a nice spreadable texture. This makes enough to cover one cake.

Serves Eight

Long Island Iced Tea

What the Harvey Wallbanger was to the bar scene on the West Coast, Long Island Iced Tea was to the East Coast. Not surprisingly, it wasn't long before each coast discovered the other's drink of choice. John Mariani credits this insidious blend of generally colorless spirits and Coca-Cola to bartender Robert "Rosebud" Butt of the Oak Beach Inn of Hampton Bays on Long Island, who supposedly created the thing in 1976. If so, Butt has much to answer for; this is a particularly lethal drink. Though it doesn't taste like iced tea, the flavor of the spirits is well concealed. It sneaks up on you and nails you between the eyes.

---

* **1 shot tequila**
* **1 shot light rum**
* **1 shot vodka**
* **1 shot gin**
* **1 dash Triple Sec**
* **1 splash sour mix**
* **Coca-Cola**
* **lemon slice**

Pour over ice in a Collins glass. Stir. Drink with caution.

Serves One

Pasta Primavera

One of the most popular upscale Italian dishes of the seventies, eighties and nineties, it is, as is often the case, virtually unknown in Italy. It was first made by the ebullient Sirio Maccioni of New York's Le Cirque Restaurant on October 2, 1975. And though what Maccioni made was a very specific mixture of zucchini, broccoli, snow peas, baby peas, asparagus, mushrooms, tomatoes and pine nuts, the multitude of imitators that followed have forced a definition of pasta primavera ("springtime") as any pasta tossed with vegetables. One of the pleasures of this dish is to use whatever is in season, especially in California, where fresh, locally grown vegetables tend to be available all year long. Though what follows is a good basic recipe, almost any combination of vegetables will do — and often has.

---

* 1/3 cup fresh peas
* 1/3 cup haricots verts
* 1/3 cup baby asparagus
* 1/3 cup mushrooms
* 1/3 cup red and green bell peppers
* 1/3 cup zucchini
* 1/3 cup broccoli
* 1/4 cup sweet butter
* 1 cup cream
* 1 tablespoon pine nuts
* 1 pound pasta (any sort will do; I'm partial to penne)
* grated Parmesan cheese to taste
* salt and pepper to taste

Thinly slice all of the vegetables and saute them in butter. Add the cream, salt and pepper, and stir briskly. Cook the pasta, drain, toss with the vegetables and pine nuts, and sprinkle with Parmesan cheese.

Serves Four

Mushroom Quiche

My personal quiche favorite from the seventies is the always palatable mushroom quiche. Real men do eat quiche. And they drink some good Vouvray to wash it down.

---

* 1 unbaked 9-inch pie shell
* 2 tablespoons butter
* 1/2 pound sliced mushrooms
* 3 minced scallions
* 1 teaspoon minced garlic
* pinch marjoram
* pinch paprika
* 1/2 cup grated Gruyere cheese
* 1/4 cup grated Parmesan cheese
* 2 eggs
* 1/2 cup cream
* pinch nutmeg
* 2 tablespoons chopped parsley
* salt and pepper
* 1/2 cup mozzarella

Saute the mushrooms, scallions and garlic in butter until soft, then mixing in the marjoram and paprika.

Scatter the cheeses on the bottom of the pie crust. Pour the mushroom mixture over the cheese. Mix the eggs, cream, salt and pepper, nutmeg and parsley together in a bowl, and pour over the mushroom mixture. Top with the mozzarella. Bake at 375 degrees for 40 minutes. Serve with salad.

Serves Four

White Chocolate Mousse

I'd be remiss to not acknowledge that one of the culinary trends of the seventies was a sudden explosion of white chocolate desserts. I've never been a fan of most the white chocolate cakes, (the somewhat contradictory) white chocolate brownies or white chocolate truffles. But a white chocolate mousse invented by Chef Michel Fitoussi of New York's Palace Restaurant in 1977 is surprisingly palatable. His recipe requires using a candy thermometer and heating a sugar mixture to 250 degrees — a sure road to perdition and a kitchen that will need repainting after trying it. My version is a lot simpler, thanks to the wonders of unflavored gelatin.

---

* **1/2 cup sugar**
* **1 teaspoon unflavored gelatin dissolved in 1 tablespoon water**
* **6 ounces white chocolate, cut into small pieces**
* **3 cups heavy cream**
* **4 egg whites**
* **1/2 cup confectioners sugar**
* **2 teaspoons vanilla**

Mix the sugar with the dissolved unflavored gelatin. Melt the chocolate in half of the cream. Mix the remaining cream with the confectioners sugar, the egg whites and vanilla, and whip vigorously. Combine in a serving bowl, and chill.

Serve topped with the berry sauce of your choice.

Serves Four

Shindler's Quintessential Chili

Whatever the origin, the point of chili is that it can be made out of just about anything. Like religion and politics, nobody agrees about the one true chili. Some argue for chunks of beef, while others insist the beef must be ground. Some say beans, especially red kidney beans (as in Cincinnati-style chili) are perfectly appropriate; others rail that beans are simply cheap filler. Some say chili must be Simon pure, while others argue for the presence of lamb, mutton, cinnamon, chicken, duck — God knows what else. What I don't know is that it goes great with beer. And that it tastes even better the next day, and better still the day after that. And in the seventies, after the divisions and social turmoil of the sixties, it can well be argued that it was chili — made en masse and cooked by all — that helped bring us back together.

---

* 3 pounds flank steak, cut into small cubes
* 2 pounds boned chicken parts, especially dark meat
* 2 pounds smoky links, sliced into small chunks
* 3 10-ounce cans chicken broth
* 48 ounces canned stewed tomatoes
* 2 7-ounce cans diced green chili peppers
* 1/4 cup minced garlic
* 1/2 cup Gebhardt's Chili Powder (or equivalent)
* 1 tablespoon dry oregano
* 2 tablespoons brown sugar
* 1 bottle Mexican beer
* 1 pound grated Monterey Jack cheese
* 2 cups chopped onions
* 2 cups chopped green and red bell peppers
* 1/4 cup lime juice
* 1 shot tequila

Combine all ingredients up to and including the beer in a large pot and cook for two hours. Add the onions and peppers, and cook for another four hours. Just before serving, add the cheese to thicken mixture (it works far better than you might think). Add the lime juice and tequila. Stir well.

Serves Twenty-four

The Bonfire of the Eateries
1980~1990

The question that drove the eighties was, What really matters? Health? Wealth? Or not overcooking the fish? The answer, I suspect, involved the fish. For it was in the eighties that the foodie movement, born in the seventies, came into full bloom. It was a decade when more than a few otherwise intelligent souls would have gladly argued that the single most important invention since the wheel was the Cuisinart. When people actually knew what a sauce spoon looked like and how to use it. When serious debates broke out over what wine went best with Chinese food. (Light, fruity whites are best, like sauvignon blanc and Johannisberg riesling, though beer is even better.)

It was a decade when a lot of us spent an amazing amount of money on foodstuff that was more for show than for actual consumption. I knew more than a few people with cupboards full of fifty-dollar bottles of first-pressing extra virgin olive oils and two-hundred-fifty-dollar bottles of balsamic vinegar, none of which they actually opened. It was the decade of exceedingly obscure olives, picked and pickled in towns high in the Pyrenees that only goats knew of. The decade of vintage sardines (thanks to the olive oil in which the sardines are packed), of refrigerators full of stone crocks of French mustard thicker than mud, of mushroom ketchup, cloth bags of whole nutmegs, bottles of capers, an assortment of filé gumbo powder and enough brands of honey, jams and preserves to supply Buckingham Palace's teas for a year. It was the decade of the kiwi.

In the eighties, many of us paid a lot of money for remarkably small amounts of food in restaurants. Nouvelle cuisine and cuisine minceur trickled down from the temples of haute cuisine to restaurants where regular folks ate. And regular folks were not thrilled by the experience. Being charged twice as much for half as much food because the salad was made of mache and mesclun and the lamb was free-range and buttermilk-fed did very little for real appetites. One notable restaurant served an appetizer consisting of a tortilla chip cut into the shape of an arrow, decorated with about half a teaspoon of green sauce and about half a teaspoon of red sauce. There wasn't enough food on the plate to feed a parakeet. The restaurant thoughtfully didn't charge for it. Most of the rest of its dishes weren't much bigger — and the restaurant charged plenty of money for them.

The good news about the decade of the foodie was that foodies were notoriously fickle creatures who always wanted to be on the cutting edge of whatever was new at that exact moment. Which meant that if you didn't especially like one culinary trend, you just gave it a few minutes and it would go away, to be replaced by yet another trend of equal transitoriness.

Thus, before the decade was half over, French cooking was on the run, laughed out of town because of one too many orders of foie gras hidden under a slice of carrot. It was replaced, in turn, by the Ethiopian trend, the Cajun trend, the Southwestern trend, the Tapas trend, the God-bless-America trend, the California pizza trend and, as the decade drew to an end, the return-to-French-cuisine-as-long-as-it's-bistro-food trend, among others. And, of course, sushi became more popular than ever.

The Ethiopian trend — a blip, really — was pure foodie heaven, a cuisine of marvelous obscurity eaten using a sort of bread called *injera* that bears a striking resemblance to a washcloth. At least one restaurant critic declared it the next big thing. At least one other expressed shock that people would go to Ethiopian restaurants while people in Ethiopia were going to bed hungry — a circuitous bit of illogic worthy of the Reagan White House. (Because there were hungry people in Ethiopian, Ethiopian restaurateurs should be put out of business?)

The Cajun thing was a lot more powerful, moved along by the remarkably large Paul Prudhomme, a terrible role model for his cooking (he weighed well over 300 pounds) but a remarkable chef. At K-Paul's Louisiana Kitchen, Prudhomme served awesomely spiced blackened redfish, Cajun popcorn and the like. It was akin to a religious revival for the taste buds, a dazzling array of high intensity tastes that foodies adored and non-foodies found satisfying as well. Thanks to Prudhomme, restaurants all across America began churning out blackened this and blackened that. I can recall going to a branch of the Cheesecake Factory chain and encountering blackened salmon, a very bad idea. I also came across blackened spaghetti at an Italian place that thought this a good bandwagon to leap on. The dish didn't even approach inedible. Unfortunately, the oversaturation of the market soon killed off this particular trend (though a variant did make a comeback in the nineties, thanks to the energetic cooking of N'Awlins chef Emeril Lagasse).

The Southwestern trend of the eighties was significantly less loved. There was good cooking to be found in the kitchens of chefs like Mark Miller of Coyote Cafe in Santa Fe; Dean Fearing of the Mansion on Turtle Creek in Dallas and Stephen Pyles of Star Canyon in Dallas. But, when the food trickled down to the rest of us, it consisted mostly of Tex-Mex dishes made with blue-corn tortillas. It came and went very quickly, though it did leave behind a lot of exotic drinks made with tequila, as well as a lot of exotic tequilas that cost fifty dollars a bottle and up — a lot of money for what was once regarded as south-of-the-border bellywash.

The Tapas trend, a movement that supposedly had all of us eating small Spanish snacks and sipping fine pale sherry, existed more in the minds of America's cooking magazines than in the real world. A few places opened (and closed) in New York and Los Angeles. Cafe Ba-Ba-Reeba

survived in Chicago, thanks more to restaurateur Richard Melman's showmanship than to Chicago's love of *camarones a la plancha* and manchego cheese. Anyway, such a trend was doomed from the start, for far too many people thought tapas had something to do with topless, especially since they were served in places called tapas bars. I suggested once that someone might consider opening a topless tapas bar, but the idea never seemed to take off.

Since the culinary pendulum swings like mad, it was no surprise in the eighties that we went from the tiny portions of nouvelle cuisine back to the massive portions of God-bless-America chow — chicken-fried steak, meat loaf, chili, hamburgers and the like, all cooked to perfection by upscale chefs in upscale restaurants at upscale prices. At a spot in Los Angeles called the West Beach Cafe, a beef taco plate went on the menu for twenty-four dollars. At the 21 Club in New York, people also paid twenty-four dollars for the privilege of chewing on Anne Rosenzweig's hamburger. At 72 Market Street in Venice, California, celebrities vied for reservations that would allow them to chow down on kick-ass

chili. The rest of America looked on in wonder as the trendier magazines extolled the revival of casserole and pot pie, neither of which had ever disappeared from ordinary restaurants.

And to everyone's surprise, by the time the decade was over, French food had reappeared, chiefly as a result of the God-bless-America trend. If we could eat trencherman American dishes, we could consume trencherman French dishes as well, especially those found at the great bistros of Paris. The cuisine of choice became rotisserie grilled chicken with big piles of really crispy French fries, pot-au-feu, cassoulet, bouillabaisse, moules à la marinière and the like. Cheap wines made a comeback as well. Kir, a brief foodie affection, was banished. More than a few of us wondered if there was anyplace to get absinthe.

All told, in the eighties, far too many of us had more money than sense. In the decade that followed, we had far less money, though still not a lot of sense. What we did have was a dreadful fear of our high-density lipoprotein, low-density lipoprotein and triglyceride levels. The eighties were the last big party of the century. In the nineties, across the board, we were to pay for our sins. ★

Blackened Redfish

In 1984, New Orleans chef Paul Prudhomme put out his cookbook titled Chef Paul Prudhomme's Louisiana Kitchen. *And in one fell swoop, he changed our national perception of the cooking in N'Awlins forever. Where the buzz dishes had been gumbo and jambalaya, they were now blackened redfish, Cajun popcorn, jalapeño cheese bread, tasso and oysters in cream on pasta and fish with pecan butter sauce. In an age of thin, this was food that was unabashedly full of butter, cream and bacon. Starved for rich flavors, we took to it like a mackerel in the Mojave takes to a bucket of water. We dove right in, head first.*

If you want to try it at home, the following recipe is a simplification of Prudhomme's (rather than making his seasoning mix from scratch, I've opted to use his bottled seasoning, I've condensed the cooking process by a few steps). Do note — making this dish can mess up your stove something awful.

---

* **1 pound butter**
* **1 bottle Paul Prudhomme's Cajun Magic Powder (or a combination of paprika, salt, onion powder, garlic powder, cayenne, white pepper, black pepper, thyme and oregano, mixed to taste)**
* **1 pound firm-fleshed fish filets (redfish if possible, otherwise red snapper, pompano, sea bass or even salmon)**

As Prudhomme points out, it's vital to heat a large cast-iron skillet as hot as you can. Melt the butter in a smaller pan and dip the fish filets in the butter, then in the spice mixture, making sure to coat the fish on both sides. Boldly drop the filets into the hot skillet one at a time, dabbing a little butter on top. Cook until blackened on the bottom, turn over and anoint with more melted butter. Expect the fish to cook extremely fast; be careful to blacken, but not incinerate, it.

Serves Four

Cajun Popcorn

Prudhomme actually contributed two great dishes to the cooking of America in the eighties, both of which were widely imitated (though his original recipes were rarely equaled). Cajun popcorn was, and still is, a sports bar favorite, a brilliant variation on calamari fritti using crayfish, shrimp or crabmeat instead of squid. It also introduced America to the very pleasant concept of remoulade sauce. It's hard not to finish every last drop. (Once again, I've simplified Prudhomme's original recipe by using his commercial seasoning mix and by condensing some of the steps. And once again, this is a dish that can make hash of your kitchen when the oil starts flying.)

---

* 2 eggs
* 1-1/2 cups milk
* 1/2 cup all-purpose flour
* 1 teaspoon sugar
* 1 bottle Paul Prudhomme's Cajun Magic Powder (or a combination of salt, onion powder, garlic powder, cayenne, white pepper, black pepper, thyme and basil, mixed to taste)
* 2 pounds small shrimp (or crayfish tails if available)

Remoulade Sauce

* 2 cups mayonnaise
* 2 tablespoons Creole mustard
* 2 tablespoons horseradish
* 2 tablespoons Worcestershire sauce
* 1 tablespoon Tabasco sauce
* 1 teaspoon minced garlic
* 1 teaspoon white vinegar
* 2 tablespoons ketchup

In a bowl, beat together the eggs and milk, then add the flour, sugar and seasoning. Let the mixture rest. Heat the oil in a heavy skillet, coat the seafood with the batter, and deep-fry until it's crispy and brown. Drain on paper towels.

To make the sauce, blend all ingredients in a blender till smooth. Dip the Cajon Popcorn in this liberally.

Serves Four

Salmon and Golden Caviar Pizza

In 1982, Wolfgang Puck opened Spago in West Hollywood and tout le Hollywood showed up to eat exotic salads, surprisingly simple pastas and a breed of pizza that came to be known as California pizzas. As perceived by Puck, it's a bracingly crisp pie topped variously with duck sausage, lamb sausage, goat cheese, smoked salmon, golden caviar, sun-dried tomatoes and much more. The quickest way to taste it, aside from going to Spago or one of the Wolfgang Puck Cafes, is to buy a Wolfgang Puck frozen pizza at the market; it's easily the best frozen pizza around, and comes back to life with remarkable verve. Otherwise, I suggest buying ready-made pizza crust and topping it in a wildly Puckish fashion.

---

* ★ **ready-made pizza dough (available at most markets)**
* ★ **1/4 pound smoked salmon**
* ★ **4 tablespoons olive oil**
* ★ **6 tablespoons sour cream**
* ★ **4 tablespoons golden caviar**
* ★ **minced chives**

Spread out the pizza dough and brush it with olive oil. Bake on a pizza stone in a 500 degree oven for ten minutes. Top with sour cream, slices of salmon and golden caviar. Garnish with minced chives. Slice and serve.

Serves Two

Crab Cakes

Ever since the twenties, and possibly earlier, the denizens of Baltimore's Lexington Market have feasted on grand and glorious deep-fried patties of crab and crackers known simply as crab cakes. Oddly, it took a while for the gospel of the crab cake to travel to the rest of us. But when it did, in the 1980s, every restaurant that could get its hands on lump crabmeat began making the things. And many restaurants that couldn't get crabmeat gave it a try as well; there are more than a few crab cakes out there made out of everything but crab. There's much disagreement as to whether the true crab cake is made with cracker crumbs or bread crumbs. In either case, it should be large, crisp and packed with identifiable bits of crabmeat. It shouldn't be crisp within, but it shouldn't be watery and mushy either. When it's mushy within, it usually means only a small bit of crab is used.

---

* 2 cups lump crabmeat
* 1 scallion, finely chopped
* 1 tablespoon minced green bell pepper
* 1 tablespoon minced red bell pepper
* 1/2 cup cracker crumbs
* 1 tablespoon mayonnaise
* 1 teaspoon dry mustard
* 2 eggs
* 1 tablespoon minced parsley
* 1 teaspoon Worcestershire sauce
* 1 dash Tabasco
* salt and pepper to taste
* butter

In a bowl, combine all of the ingredients except the butter. Work into medium-size patties. Melt the butter in a large, heavy skillet. Fry the patties until they're crisp and more than golden brown on each side. Keep adding butter to make them as brown as can be. Serve with tartar sauce.

Serves Six

Crème Brûlée

Depending on whom you choose to believe, crème brûlée ("burnt cream") is either a popular British dish of the seventeenth century, a popular French dish of the nineteenth century, a popular Cajun dish from the turn of the century or a variation brought to America from Spain by Chef Alain Sailhac or his boss, Sirio Maccioni, of Le Cirque (who's also credited with inventing pasta primavera). In any case, the dish became a sensation at New York's Le Cirque beginning in 1982. It was picked up almost instantly by several thousand restaurants from New York to Los Angeles. In the years since, crème brûlée has been made with chocolate and butterscotch and filled with berries. It's been turned into an upscale version of My-T-Fine pudding. The best is the original — simple and to the point.

---

* **4 cups whipping cream**
* **1/4 teaspoon vanilla extract**
* **pinch salt**
* **8 egg yolks**
* **1/4 teaspoon nutmeg**
* **7/8 cup sugar**
* **8 tablespoons brown sugar**

Combine the cream, vanilla and salt in a saucepan, warm on a flame for five minutes. In a bowl, mix together the egg yolks, nutmeg and sugar. Pour in the cream, and stir to combine. Pour into eight 3/4 cup ramekins (available at your local ramekin shop), place in about an inch of water in a roasting pan, and stick in a 300 degree oven. Loosely cover with foil, and bake for an hour, or until set. Remove from the oven, and refrigerate until ready to use. Then top each ramekin with one tablespoon brown sugar and either melt it under broiler or caramelize with a blowtorch (available at your local welding shop).

Serves Eight

Fajitas

Fajitas became downright ubiquitous in the eighties, thanks in part to its constant mention during the 1984 Republican Presidential Convention in Dallas. One school of thought insists that fajitas were born in San Antonio, a major center of fajitas consumption. The dish may have gotten there from Mexico, where a similar preparation is called arrechera. *Or it may have evolved with Mexican ranch hands working in the Southwest, who simply combined Mexican cooking styles with American ingredients — very much like chop suey. Whatever the case, beef is the basic ingredient, though chicken and shrimp have joined it in the skillet. (We will not discuss oddities like moo shu fajitas, fajita pitas and potato skins filled with fajitas.) The basic fajita is made using strips of marinated steak, cooked in a heavy black skillet with sliced onions and green peppers, served still sizzling with side orders of rice, beans, guacamole and tortillas.*

---

* **2 pounds skirt or flank steak**
* **1/2 cup lime juice**
* **1/3 cup vegetable oil**
* **1/3 cup tequila**
* **2 tablespoons minced garlic**
* **1 teaspoon ground cumin**
* **1 teaspoon dried oregano**
* **1/2 teaspoon black pepper**
* **4 onions sliced in half**
* **refried beans**
* **flour tortillas**
* **salsa fresca**
* **guacamole**
* **sour cream**
* **fresh cilantro**

Slice the meat into long thin strips. Combine the lime, oil, tequila, garlic, cumin, oregano and pepper, then toss with the meat until it's well coated. Add onion halves. Cover and refrigerate overnight.

In a large, hot skillet, fry the meat and onions with marinade until they're brown and bubbly. Remove to serving plates. Serve with the refried beans, tortillas, salsa, guacamole, sour cream and cilantro.

Serves Eight

Kiwi Parfait

One day they were known as Chinese gooseberries and nobody was much interested in them. Then, in 1962, Frieda Caplan of Frieda's Finest Produce in Los Angeles began importing them from New Zealand and marketing them as kiwifruit. By the seventies, they were an intrinsic element in nouvelle cuisine. By the eighties, they were everywhere, even in fruit salads in chain restaurants. The odd little Chinese gooseberry, with its fuzzy exterior and intense green interior, had become a part of American cuisine.

* **1 cup cold milk**
* **1 cup sour cream**
* **1/4 teaspoon almond extract**
* **1 package Jell-O Vanilla Instant Pudding**
* **1 cup peeled, sliced kiwifruit**

In a bowl, combine the milk, sour cream and almond extract. Add the pudding mix and beat well with an electric mixer. Layer the pudding and kiwi slices in parfait glasses. Chill at least one hour. Garnish with whipped cream.

Serves Six

Sushi

Much like a mass religious conversion, a whole generation decided that not only was seafood healthy, it was especially healthy if eaten raw. Sushi bars flourished in our major cities. Otherwise persnickety diners came to know the difference between sea eel and freshwater eel, and the subtleties of the California roll. And the more adventurous also discovered that simple sushi dishes were fun to make at home — though deep-fried soft-shell crab rolls are best left to the experts.

---

* **short-grained rice (available at most Asian markets)**
* **the absolute best, freshest fish you can find (tuna is a good choice)**
* **Seasoned rice vinegar**
* **1 small can wasabi (Japanese horseradish)**

Cook the rice per the instructions (a Japanese electric rice steamer is a fine investment if you want to get serious about your sushi). Remove all bones and filaments from the fish, and carefully slice it into elegant rhomboids. Lightly toss the rice with a small amount of flavored rice vinegar. Make small pillows of the rice. Mix wasabi powder with water as per instructions to make a greenish paste. Top with a dab of the wasabi, then carefully place a slice of fish on top. Wash down with lots of hot sake.

Serves Four

Ranch Dressing

The leading salad dressing of the eighties, as well as the primary dip of the decade, was supposedly born at Hidden Valley Ranch, near Santa Barbara, California. Hidden Valley Ranch Original Ranch Dressing mix, a California cult item for years, was made by adding buttermilk to the contents of the package. It was served at chain restaurants with everything from onion rings and deep-fried mushrooms to actual lettuce. Though you can buy it ready-made in bottles, it still tastes better if you mix the powder with the buttermilk according to the package's directions. If you insist on doing it yourself, though, try the following recipe.

---

* **1 cup mayonnaise**
* **1 cup buttermilk**
* **2 teaspoons dried parsley flakes**
* **2 tablespoons chopped scallions**
* **1/4 teaspoon onion powder**
* **1/2 teaspoon minced garlic**
* **pinch cayenne pepper**
* **salt and pepper to taste**

Combine all ingredients in a bowl, chill and serve.

Serves Four

Couch Potato Meat Loaf Sandwich

In the eighties, meat loaf, of all things, became trendy. It was helped along by places like 72 Market Street in Venice, California, to which Hollywood heavy-weights drove in their Porsche Carreras to order the all-American dish. To make a proper meat loaf at home is a no brainer. You must have some sort of meat, probably ground. You must have some sort of starchy thing, like bread or pota-toes, to keep the meat molecules from bumping into each other. And you must have some sort of glue, usually eggs because eggs are an even more powerful adhesive than epoxy. These elements are found in this perfectly wonderful recipe.

* 3 pounds ground meat (beef and pork are a good combination, toss in some turkey or sausage)
* 1 tablespoon minced garlic
* 2 medium onions, minced
* 1 green bell pepper, coarsely chopped
* 2 eggs
* 1/2 teaspoon dried oregano
* 1/4 teaspoon paprika
* 1/4 teaspoon dried dill
* 1 teaspoon honey
* 2 cups bread crumbs
* 1/2 cup grated Parmesan cheese
* 1 8-ounce can tomato sauce
* 1/2 cup milk
* salt and pepper to taste
* 1/2 cup ketchup
* mayonnaise
* white bread

Mix all ingredients except the ketchup together in a big bowl. This works best if you just mash everything together with your hands. Push it all into a loaf pan, pour the ketchup on top, put the pan in the oven and bake it at 350 degrees for an hour and a half to make sure all the toxins are destroyed. Let it cool, then whack the sides and bottom until the loaf falls out, preferably onto a plate and not the floor. Slice and eat on white bread, thickly spread with mayonnaise and ketchup.

Serves Twelve

Guilty Pleasures and Lean Cuisine
1990~2000

I don't know about you, but I've spent much of the nineties eating chicken. Mind you, I like chicken a good deal. Especially chicken that's cooked on a rotisserie for a long, slow time, anointed with oils, coated with herbs, redolent of garlic. The sort of chicken where the bones just slip right on out and the meat is as moist as if it were dipped in butter. In Los Angeles, where I live, we ate Cuban chicken at Versailles, Armenian chicken at Zankou, healthy chicken (skinless) at Koo Koo Roo, Mexican chicken at El Pollo Loco, country chicken at Kenny Rogers Roasters, New England chicken at Boston Market, California chicken at the California Chicken Cafe. There's Japanese chicken at Kokkekokko, Chinese chicken at Sam Woo's, Peruvian chicken at El Pollo Inka, Italian chicken at Rosti and so many more. At certain points in the decade, I felt as if I were beginning to sprout feathers.

It's significant that chicken was one of the prime dishes of the decade, for the nineties were, on one level, a return to reality, and on another level, an era of diminished expectations. In *Fashionable Food*, Sylvia Lovegren suggests that the defining cuisine of the nineties was *cucina povera*, or the cuisine of poverty, defined by a national obsession with beans. I guess. Myself, except for noting a certain beaniness among the Oldways folks, who are fond of re-creating the cuisine of pre-Columbians, Peruvians and the like, I didn't observe any obsessions with beans. Looking at my cupboard shelves, I didn't see any at all. I rather like barbecued beans with my ribs and hot links, but that's about as far as my involvement with *cucina povera* goes.

In fact, the *nostalgie de la boue* that began to appear in the upper middle class in the sixties really flourished in the nineties. More time than ever was spent discussing the relative merits of a bowl of chili versus a BLT. *Seinfeld* made mass-produced breakfast cereal fashionable again — not granola, but the stuff flavored with freeze-dried marshmallows in the shape of body parts. Coffee — formerly a cheap cup o' joe — was everywhere, amazingly resisting a howling mass of stand-up comedy routines about the silliness of half-caf, half-espresso with nonfat foam on the top. And the ubiquity of coffee was obvious in an age of goggle-eyed, Net-surfing late-night madness — if you wanted to cruise the Web at four in the morning, there was nothing like a double latte to keep your eyes pinned open.

In the nineties, really low-rent alcoholic beverages went upscale. Who would possibly imagine that mescal, crude and raw, would become a gourmet's delight in the decade, with bottles of extra primo mescal (sans the worm) going for more than a fat, oaky Chardonnay? Tequila became trendier than ever, though many of us wondered whether we were paying for the beverage or the bottle when we bought Patròn Gold and Patròn Silver.

And it was in the nineties that we the people (and especially we the baby boomers) went into complete and total vapor lock when it came to cholesterol. Frankly, like many of my generation, I lived in mortal fear of sudden death, especially after a decade of being badgered by the forces of good health about the morbid dangers of cholesterol. On the other hand, though I don't mean to minimize the issue, the reams of chatter involving all the unhealthy goo, glop, sludge and muck clogging our bloodstreams reminded me of a point the great journalist A.J. Liebling made back in 1959 in his culinary reminiscence *Between Meals: An Appetite for Paris*. He wrote:

> In the heroic age before the First World War, there were men and women who ate, in addition to a whacking lunch and a glorious dinner, a voluminous supper after the theater or the other amusements of the evening. I have known some of the survivors, octogenarians of unblemished appetite and unfailing good humor — spry, wry, and free of the ulcers that come from worrying about a balanced diet — but they have had no emulators in France since the doctors there discovered the existence of the human liver.

Liebling goes on to detail the lives of a number of great eaters of the old school, who could really pack it away and wash it down with wine in copious quantities. All of them seemed to live to ripe old ages, and all of them continued to consume the richest of the rich dishes of France with no problems at all. Often, their ends came as a result of being run over by a car at age ninety-four on their way to dinner. The point is, quite clearly, that we were a lot healthier before the discovery of the liver led us to believe that we weren't healthy at all.

Liebling's thesis would, no doubt, hold up a lot better were it not for the unfortunate fact that Liebling himself died in 1963 at the age of fifty-nine, racked with gout, the result of a life of massive self-indulgence at the table. Still, I think there is a point to be made here: sometimes problems don't actually exist until we're told that they exist. People lived to ripe old ages before cholesterol testing became the Pet Rock of the late twentieth century, and it's perfectly possible that worrying about your cholesterol level has the result of raising the level that you're worrying about.

People of the boomer persuasion used to talk about nothing but the appreciation of their real estate; in the late nineties, they amended those numbers with extensive annotations on the state of their cholesterol. And not just their cholesterol, but also their HDL, LDL and triglyceride levels, along with their all-important cholesterol/HDL ratio.

Unfortunately, there wasn't much we could do about it but worry. I didn't eat more than a few eggs a week. I didn't spread butter on my bread. I ate a lot more fish and poultry than meat. I trudged three miles a day. I did all the right things. My weight was finally under control. And yet, thanks to my fear of cholesterol (have you heard? there's a new home-testing unit for cholesterol — what fun!), I felt that I was a mess. My cupboard was filled with products that declare in bold type, **no cholesterol**. The good news, I suppose, was that I wasn't worried about my liver at all. But then, compared with the morbid consequences of cholesterol, the liver ailments so popular half a century ago seemed like a low-fat picnic in the park.

Ultimately, it was been a decade of simplification and *reductio ad cuisinum*. Most folks I knew, ate pretty casual meals. Thanks to the scare tactics of the food police at the Center for Science in the Public Interest, a lot of us spent the decade running around like headless chickens (the chicken motif again), living in mortal fear of Chinese food, Italian food, Mexican food, fast food, muffins and sweet buns — even popcorn for the luv o' Mike!

Everywhere we turned, culinary bogeymen popped out of the woodwork, darkly intoning warnings about the dangers of eating butter, margarine, animal products, anything with fat of any kind, anything with salt, anything with taste and flavor. It was a decade of low-fat buffalo meat, low-fat beefalo meat, low-fat ostrich meat, low-fat turkey burger, low-fat veggie burgers. Aging boomers, feeling their first twinges of mortality, were convinced that just a single spoonful of refried beans cooked with lard would have them

pushing up daisies in no time. Mickey D's gave us the McLean Deluxe, and Taco Bell came out with its Taco Bell Lite line of low-fat dishes. Snackwell's cookies were all the rage. It was a downright monastic decade. Culinary fun was in short supply.

But it didn't disappear. It was in the nineties that blue M&Ms were born. Pizza Hut gave us the Stuffed Crust Pizza. And for the first time in history, real restaurants opened in Las Vegas, which had long been as much a culinary desert as it was a real one. America's most sinful playland became home to a Spago, a Spago Cafe, a Wolfgang Puck Cafe, a Fog City Diner, Emeril's, Coyote Cafe, Ruth's Chris Steakhouse, Z Tejas and the Palm. It even developed a small Chinatown.

But for the most part, the decade seemed to be closing with much gnashing of teeth, rending of garments and mortification of the flesh. Which is, I'm given to believe, the way most centuries come to an end. This one was a marvelous roller-coaster ride, a journey from the high formality and dietary unconsciousness of the 1900s to the high informality and intense dietary consciousness of the 1990s. If everything works as it usually does, by the year 2099, we'll be dressed-to-the-nines formal again and eating fat like it's going out of style. For better or for worse, that's how it always goes. ★

Beefalo Steak with Grilled Onions

In the nineties, all sorts of low-fat, low-cholesterol meats appeared on the market, allowing those hungry for some grilled hide to savor their beef with all the flavor but only a fraction of the guilt: beefalo (an animal that results from a cross between Herford or Charolais cattle and buffalo), buffalo and even ostrich — which, contrary to the usual assumption, doesn't taste very much like chicken. It tastes like venison — and venison is a good thing to taste like. The beefalo steak used in this recipe is available in many supermarkets throughout the country.

---

* ★ **1/2 cup olive oil**
* ★ **1/2 cup lemon juice**
* ★ **1/4 cup chopped cilantro**
* ★ **1 small onion, chopped**
* ★ **1/2 teaspoon minced garlic**
* ★ **salt and pepper to taste**
* ★ **1-1/2 pounds beefalo steak**
* ★ **1 large red onion, thickly sliced**

Combine the oil, lemon juice, cilantro, chopped onion, garlic, salt and pepper in a glass bowl. Add the steak and let marinate overnight, turning as often as possible. Grill over coals (mesquite if available) until the meat is tender. Beefalo cooks rapidly because of its low fat content. Add the sliced onions and char quickly. Slice the meat across the grain into thin strips, and serve with the onions and baked potatoes.

Serves Four

Poached Monkfish Salad with Capers

In the nineties, Americans discovered that one of the ugliest fish to ever shame the ocean also happened to be tasty. The French call it lotte. *It's also variously called an anglerfish, a goosefish, a bellyfish, a bellowsfish, a frogfish or an allmouth. Because its firm flesh tastes like that of the far more expensive crustacean, it's also known as the poor man's lobster. But the name that's used the most often is monkfish. There's a lot of very fine eating here. This is a remarkably versatile fish that can be grilled, baked, and even poached and used, as in this case, as lobster would be, in a salad.*

---

* **1/2 cup olive oil**
* **1-1/2 tablespoons vinegar**
* **1/2 teaspoon dry mustard**
* **1/2 teaspoon dry tarragon**
* **salt and pepper to taste**
* **1 pound monkfish, poached and chilled**
* **1/2 red bell pepper, seeded and julienned**
* **1/2 green bell pepper, seeded and julienned**
* **4 thinly sliced scallions**
* **2 tablespoons capers**
* **1/2 teaspoon green peppercorns**
* **mesclun**

In a bowl, mix together the oil, vinegar, mustard, tarragon, salt and pepper. Slice the fish and toss with the dressing. In a salad bowl, compose the peppers, scallions, capers, peppercorns and mesclun. Top with the fish and vinaigrette.

Serves Four

Rice Pudding

As the euphoria of the eighties came to a startling end, rice pudding began appearing on restaurant menus around the country. It was often tricked up a bit to make it seem more modern — made with dried cranberries or basmati rice or something like that. But it was still rice pudding, the ultimate soothing dessert, the edible balm that made life seem worth living, even as the world crashed down about us. But at least we could sit down in front of the television set and eat rice pudding and feel that someone cared.

* **1/2 cup cooked rice**
* **1/2 teaspoon salt**
* **2-1/2 cups boiling water**
* **3-1/2 cups milk**
* **3 eggs**
* **1/2 cup cream**
* **1/3 cup sugar**
* **2 teaspoons vanilla**
* **1/2 cup plump golden raisins**
* **2 tablespoons melted butter**
* **cinnamon**

Cook the rice in salted boiling water for fifteen minutes. Drain, then combine rice and milk. Beat the eggs with the cream, then add the sugar, vanilla, raisins and butter. Mix with rice and milk. Pour into a two-quart casserole and bake in a water bath at 300 degrees for twenty-five minutes. Sprinkle with cinnamon to taste. Serve hot or cold, as you wish.

Serves Six

Risotto with Fresh Mushrooms and Dried Porcini

It was a very good decade for rice. Not only did we return to rice pudding, we also went fairly mad for arborio rice, the uniquely wondrous rice from Italy's fertile Po Valley used to make risotto. The really nice thing about risotto is that because it's built around rice, it gives the illusion of being a diet dish — kind of like sushi but with an Italian twist. Though it can be a diet dish, it usually isn't. In fact, after you add all that butter, olive oil and cream, it's anything but.

---

* **4 cups chicken broth**
* **1/2 cup white wine**
* **1 small package dried porcini**
* **4 ounces sliced fresh mixed mushrooms**
* **4 tablespoons butter**
* **2 tablespoons olive oil**
* **1/4 cup minced onions**
* **1 tablespoon minced garlic**
* **2 cups uncooked arborio rice**
* **1/4 cup cream**
* **1/2 cup Parmesan cheese**
* **1 tablespoon chopped fresh cilantro**

Bring the broth to a boil, lower to a simmer, add the white wine and the mushrooms, and cook for five minutes. Heat the butter and oil in a heavy casserole, add the onion and garlic and saute until soft. Add the rice, stirring until it's well coated. Add the broth, a little at a time, stirring constantly, waiting until it's absorbed before adding more. Cook over low heat, stirring often, for twenty minutes. Then add the cream, Parmesan and cilantro, and stir vigorously. Cook until thickened.

Serves Six

Turkey Burger

It's not surprising that the evil old hamburger was replaced (for many, but certainly not for all) with the more benign turkey burger, an affable creation that can, in a pinch, be rather wonderful. It's a dish that suffers from flavor deficit disorder (FDD). You've got to add a fair amount of herbs and spices to make it taste really good.

---

* **1 pound ground turkey meat (all breast if you want it to be really low in fat and cholesterol)**
* **2 eggs**
* **1 tablespoon minced garlic**
* **1/4 cup finely chopped onion**
* **1/4 teaspoon Worcestershire sauce**
* **1/2 tablespoon ketchup**
* **1 tablespoon bread crumbs**
* **pinch dried oregano**
* **pinch dried thyme**
* **salt and pepper to taste**

In a bowl, mix all ingredients by hand. Form into nice plump burgers. Charcoal grill until brown on both sides, by which time they should be cooked through. Serve on soft onion rolls with whatever condiments your heart desires.

Serves Four

Garbanzo Bean Veggie Burger

The meatless burger, an abomination to some, a statement concerning the future necessities of the world to others, is not always the tastiest of creations. (It can be, with sufficient verve, herbs and spices.) There's no denying that it did become one of the defining dishes of the nineties — even McDonald's was rumored to have one in development. I've tried a lot of them and find some of the store-bought models fairly palatable — especially the ones made from mushrooms, and the original and actual Vegeburger. If you want to make one from scratch, try the following. But be prepared to add a fair amount of salt and pepper to make it taste really good.

---

* **2 cups mashed garbanzo beans**
* **1 stalk celery, minced**
* **1 carrot, finely minced**
* **1/2 small onion, minced**
* **1/4 cup bread crumbs**
* **1 egg**
* **1/4 teaspoon curry powder**
* **1/4 teaspoon chili powder**
* **salt and pepper to taste**
* **cooking oil**

Mix all ingredients except the oil in bowl. Shape into six patties. Fry in oiled pan until brown on both sides. Eat on whole-wheat buns — of course.

Serves Three

Tiramisu

It used to be that we ended an Italian meal with spumoni, tortone or ricotta cheesecake. Then, in the late seventies, a dessert appeared on what must be every single upscale Italian menu in America (and many downscale ones as well) — tiramisu, whose name translates "pick-me-up." Interestingly, no two restaurants seemed to make it the same way, though it is a Venetian dish with a tradition that stretches back to the mid-nineteenth century. In its most basic form, it's sponge cake doctored with cream, liqueur, chocolate and coffee. But then, it's rarely served in its most basic form.

---

* **6 egg yolks**
* **3/4 cup sugar**
* **16 ounces mascarpone cheese**
* **1/4 cup sweet Marsala wine**
* **1/4 cup Kahlua**
* **3 cups freshly brewed espresso**
* **2 packages Italian ladyfingers**
* **1 cup heavy cream**
* **sugar to taste**
* **semisweet chocolate shavings**

To prevent the problems sometimes associated with raw eggs, coddle the eggs for two to three minutes, then refrigerate until chilled and firm. Using an electric mixer, blend the egg yolks and sugar. Add the Marsala and the mascarpone and stir until the mixture is thick and rich.

In a separate bowl, combine the espresso and the Kahlua, quickly dip the ladyfingers in the liquid until they're lightly soaked and line eight dessert goblets with them. Spoon in the mascarpone mixture, and refrigerate until it's chilled and set, about one hour.

Whip the cream with a sprinkling of sugar, then spoon on top of the goblets. Garnish with chocolate shavings.

Serves Eight

Chinese Chicken Salad

This is a Cantonese dish, the proper name for which is sow see guy, though, more often than not, it is found in Mandarin and Peking-style restaurants. It has been a cult item, every bit as popular as the other cult totems of latter-day Chinese cooking — potstickers, kung pao shrimp and sweet-and-sour soup — since the seventies. However, on the cusp of the eighties and nineties, Chinese chicken salad migrated out of Chinese restaurants and into restaurants otherwise noted for their American cooking, their California cuisine and, more often than not, their pizza and pasta. The California Pizza Kitchen chain made a perfectly decent Chinese chicken salad. The Wolfgang Puck Cafe chain made a remarkable rendition. These days, Chinese chicken salad is Chinese in name only. No, that's not fair — the taste, redolent of sesame oil and soy, is Chinese as well. But those stupid Mandarin oranges just have to go. And in my version, they have.

---

* **2 tablespoons soy sauce**
* **2 tablespoons sherry**
* **1 teaspoon sugar**
* **2 teaspoons powdered ginger**
* **2 teaspoons slivered garlic**
* **2 pounds boned chicken breast**
* **1 medium head iceberg lettuce, shredded**
* **1 bunch scallions, sliced**
* **1 bunch cilantro, chopped**
* **1/2 teaspoon dry mustard**
* **1/2 teaspoon black pepper**
* **1 tablespoon peanut oil**
* **2 tablespoons sesame oil**
* **2 tablespoons soy sauce**
* **2 tablespoons rice vinegar**
* **1 tablespoon toasted sesame seeds**

Combine the soy, sherry, sugar, ginger and garlic. Marinate the chicken in soy mixture. Broil the chicken until very brown, turning often. While the chicken cools, combine the lettuce, sliced scallions, chopped cilantro. Shred the chicken, and toss with the greens. Combine the remaining ingredients in bowl and pour over the salad. You'll notice I don't use bean threads or wonton noodles or anything like that. I like this salad as it is, with the chicken, the cilantro and the sesame oil dominating the flavor. The noodles strike me as being wholly extraneous.

Serves Eight

Shrimp Patròn

Tequila became a very expensive beverage in the nineties, thanks to new high-end brands like Patròn (Gold and Silver), Herradura Anejo, Cuervo 1800, Sauza Tres Generaciones and the like. Aside from sipping these intensely flavored tequilas, we also cooked with them. Tequila gives a lot of flavor to the dishes in which it's used. And though any fine tequila will work in this dish, it's Patròn that I'm fondest of; this is a good excuse for sippin' while you cook.

---

* **4 ounces Patròn tequila**
* **1/2 cup lime juice**
* **1 bunch cilantro, chopped**
* **2 tablespoons olive oil**
* **2 dried habañero chiles**
* **1 tablespoon brown sugar**
* **3 pounds of the largest shrimp you can find, shelled and deveined**
* **3 green bell peppers, sliced**
* **8 scallions, cut into one-inch pieces**
* **3 onions, cut into eighths**
* **salt and pepper to taste**
* **8 peeled garlic cloves**
* **slices of orange, lemon, lime, pineapple**

Combine the tequila, lime juice, cilantro, olive oil, chiles and brown sugar in a bowl. Marinate the shrimp in mixture for four or more hours. On a skewer, arrange the shrimp with the peppers, scallions, onions, garlic and fruit. Barbecue on a hot grill or barbecue until the shrimp is well done.

Serves Six

Chicken Tandoori

One of the best things anyone has ever done with chicken is the Pakistani process known as tandoori cooking, in which the marinated bird is cooked in a clay oven at around a thousand degrees. Since most of us don't have tandoors in our homes, certain shortcuts have to be taken. And this one works remarkably well.

* **1 cup plain yogurt**
* **2 tablespoons peanut oil**
* **1/2 cup chopped onions**
* **2 teaspoons minced garlic**
* **1/2 teaspoon powdered ginger**
* **1/4 cup lemon juice**
* **1/2 teaspoon ground coriander**
* **1/2 teaspoon ground cinnamon**
* **1/2 teaspoon ground cardamom**
* **1/2 teaspoon ground turmeric**
* **2 crumbled bay leaves**
* **1/2 teaspoon dried red chili pepper**
  salt and pepper to taste
* **2 pounds chicken pieces, skinned**

Combine the first fourteen ingredients, then pour over the chicken. Cover and refrigerate overnight, turning often. Place the chicken in a roasting pan, pour the marinade over it, and bake in a 400 degree oven for one hour, turning every twenty minutes. Then cook for an additional fifteen minutes until brown. Serve with rice.

Serves Four

Bibliography

Marcia Adams, *Marcia Adams' Heirloom Recipes: Yesterday's Favorites, Tomorrow's Treasures,* Clarkson Potter, New York, 1994

Bruce Aidells and Denis Kelly, *Real Beer and Good Eats: The Rebirth of America's Beer and Food Traditions,* Knopf, New York, 1992

James Beard, *The James Beard Cookbook,* Dell, New York, 1959

Vic Bergeron, *Trader Vic's Bartender's Guide,* Doubleday, New York, 1972

Anthony Dias Blue, *America's Kitchen: Traditional & Contemporary Regional Cooking: Featuring Recipes from America's Most Celebrated Chefs,* Turner Publishing, Atlanta, 1995

Anthony Dias Blue and Kathryn K. Blue, *Thanksgiving Dinner,* HarperCollins, New York, 1990

T. Coraghessan Boyle, *The Road to Wellville,* Viking, New York, 1993

Genevieve Callahan, *The New California Cook Book,* M. Barrows, New York, 1955

Julia Child, Simone Beck and Louisette Bertholle, *Mastering the Art of French Cooking,* Knopf, New York, 1961

Philip Collins, *The Art of the Cocktail: 100 Classic Cocktail Recipes,* Chronicle Books, San Francisco, 1992

Barnaby Conrad III, *The Martini: An Illustrated History of an American Classic,* Chronicle Books, San Francisco, 1995

Beth Dooley and Lucia Watson, *Savoring the Seasons of the Northern Heartland,* Knopf, New York, 1994

Clarence E. Edwords, *Bohemian San Francisco: Its Restaurants and Their Most Famous Recipes,* Paul Elder and Company, San Francisco, 1914

Fannie Farmer, *The All New Fannie Farmer Boston Cooking School Cookbook,* Bantam, New York, 1961

M.F.K. Fisher, *How to Cook a Wolf* [originally published 1942] from *The Art of Eating,* Vintage Books, New York, 1976

Bobby Flay and Joan Schwartz, *Bobby Flay's Bold American Food: More than 200 Revolutionary Recipes,* Warner Books, New York, 1994

Larry Forgione, *An American Place,* William Morrow & Co., New York, 1996

Milton Glaser and Jerome Snyder, *The Underground Gourmet Cookbook,* Simon and Schuster, New York, 1975

John and Karen Hess, *The Taste of America,* Grossman, New York, 1977

—, *Jell-O Brand Fun and Fabulous Recipes,* Beekman House, New York, 1988

Mrs. Simon Kander (Lizzie Black) and Mrs. Henry Schoenfeld, *"The Settlement" Cook Book, 1903: The Way to a Man's Heart* (first published in 1901), Applewood Books, Bedford, Massachusetts, 1996

Kay and Marshall Lee, *America's Favorites,* G.P. Putnam's Sons, New York, 1980

A.J. Liebling, *Between Meals: An Appetite for Paris,* Simon and Schuster, New York, 1962

Sylvia Lovegren, *Fashionable Food: Seven Decades of Food Fads,* Macmillan General Reference, New York, 1995

John Mariani, *America Eats Out: An Illustrated History of Restaurants, Taverns, Coffee Shops, Speakeasies and Other Establishments That Have Fed Us for 350 Years,* William Morrow, New York, 1991

John Mariani, *The Dictionary of American Food and Drink,* Hearst Books, New York, 1994

—, *Marriott Hot Shoppes Cookbook,* Parsons, Friedmann, Stephan and Rose, Boston, 1987

Paul McIlhenny, *The Tabasco Brand Cookbook: 125 Years of America's Favorite Pepper Sauce,* Clarkson Potter, New York, 1993

Ernest Matthew Mickler, *White Trash Cooking,* The Jargon Society, 1986

Joan Nathan, *Jewish Cooking in America,* Knopf, New York, 1994

Molly O'Neill, *New York Cookbook,* Workman Publishing Co., New York, 1992

Prudence Penny, *American Woman's Cookbook,* Consolidated Books, Chicago, 1956

Prudence Penny, *United States Regional Cookbook,* Consolidated Books, Chicago, 1956

Paul Prudhomme, *Chef Paul Prudhomme's Louisiana Kitchen,* William Morrow & Co., New York, 1984

Wolfgang Puck, *The Wolfgang Puck Cookbook: Recipes from Spago, Chinois and Points East and West,* Random House, New York, 1986

Will Rogers, *Will Rogers Cookbook* [revised edition], Will Rogers Cooperative Association of Will Rogers State Historic Park, Pacific Palisades, CA, 1992

Irma S. Rombauer and Marion Rombauer Becker, *Joy of Cooking,* Bobbs-Merrill, New York, 1973

Waverley Root, *Food: An Authoritative and Visual History and Dictionary of the Foods of the World,* Simon and Schuster, New York, 1980

Waverley Root and Richard de Rochemont, *Eating in America: A History,* Ecco Press, New York, 1976

Debbie Shore, Catherine Townsend and Laurie Roberge, *Home Food: 44 Great American Chefs Cook 160 Recipes on Their Night Off,* Clarkson Potter, New York, 1995

Raymond Sokolov, *Fading Feast: A Compendium of Disappearing American Regional Foods,* Farrar Strauss Giroux, New York, 1981

Lyn Stallworth and and Rod Kennedy, *The Brooklyn Cookbook,* Knopf, New York, 1991

Jane and Michael Stern, *American Gourmet: Classic Recipes, Deluxe Delights, Flambouyant Favorites and Swank "Company" Food from the '50s and '60s,* HarperCollins, New York, 1991

Jane and Michael Stern, *Real American Food: Jane and Michael Stern's Coast-to-Coast Cookbook,* Knopf, New York, 1986

Jane and Michael Stern, *Roadfood and Goodfood: Jane and Michael Stern's Coast-to-Coast Restaurant Guides,* Knopf, New York, 1986

Jane and Michael Stern, *Square Meals: A Cookbook,* Knopf, New York, 1984

Jane and Michael Stern, *A Taste of America,* Andrews and McMeel, Kansas City, 1988

Rex Stout, *The Nero Wolfe Cookbook,* Viking, New York, 1973

Alice B. Toklas, *The Alice B. Toklas Cookbook,* Harper & Row, New York, 1954

James Trager, *The Foodbook,* Grossman, New York, 1970

James Trager, *The Food Chronology: A Food Lover's Compendium of Events and Anecdotes, from Prehistory to the Present,* Henry Holt & Co., New York, 1995

Calvin Trillin, *Alice, Let's Eat: Further Adventures of a Happy Eater,* Random House, New York, 1978

Calvin Trillin, *American Fried: Adventures of a Happy Eater,* Doubleday, New York, 1974

Calvin Trillin, *Third Helpings,* Ticknor & Fields, New Haven, 1983

Calvin Trillin, *Travels With Alice,* Avon Books, New York, 1989

James Villas, *American Taste: A Celebration of Gastronomy Coast to Coast,* Arbor House, New York, 1982

Hugo Ziemann and Mrs. F.L. Gillette, *The White House Cookbook: Cooking, Toilet and Household Recipes, Menus, Dinner-Giving, Table Etiquette, Care of the Sick, Health Suggestions, Facts,* Saalfield Publishing, New York, 1901

Index

(Note: recipes and their page numbers are indicated in bold face type.)

About the Author

Merrill Shindler has written and spo-
ken about the pleasures of the palate
for most of his adult life. He is the
affably eccentric host of KABC Talk-
Radio's weekly *Dining Out with
Merrill Shindler* show, restaurant
critic for the *San Gabriel Valley*

Newspapers and the co-editor of the best-selling *Zagat Los
Angeles Restaurant Survey.* He likes to describe himself as
"Just a big ol' hungry boy," who spends his spare time try-
ing to figure out where to eat next.

Angel City Press

Angel City Press, established in 1992, is dedicated to the
publication of high-quality nonfiction gift books, including
the cookbooks *Hollywood du Jour* and *Chasen's.* Angel
City Press is located by the sea in Santa Monica, California.

About the Designers & Artist

American Dish was designed by Jeff Darnall of Samuels
Darnall & Associates in Capistrano Beach, California. The
book was produced on a Power Macintosh. Programs used
include Quark Express, Adobe Illustrator and Adobe
Photoshop. The font used in the body text and recipes is
Syntax; the font used in the chapter headings is Klang. The
book was printed by Thomson-Shore in Dexter, Michigan.

The title, chapter dates and illustrations were created by
Lisa Holtzman of Santa Monica, California. Lisa specializes
in calligraphy, hand lettering and illustration.